A Year *of* Sewing
with
Nani Iro

A Year of Sewing with Nani Iro
First Published in 2022 by Zakka Workshop, a division of World Book Media, LLC

www.zakkaworkshop.com
134 Federal Street
Salem, MA 01970 USA
info@zakkaworkshop.com

ATELIER TO NANI IRO KISETSU O MATO ICHINEN NO FUKU
All rights reserved. Copyright © Naomi Ito 2021
Original Japanese edition published by EDUCATIONAL FOUNDATION BUNKA GAKUEN BUNKA PUBLISHING BUREAU.
English language rights, translation & production by World Book Media LLC., through The English Agency (Japan) Ltd.

Publisher: Katsuhiro Hamada
Design and Text: Naomi Ito / ATELIER to nani IRO
Model: Miwako Ichikawa
Photography: Jun Okada, Jotaro Sakashita & Josui Yasuda
Styling: Setsuko Todoroki
Hair & Makeup: Hiromi Chinone
Japanese Book Design: Kei Sumiya
Pattern Production: Ai Yoshida
Sample Production: ATELIER to nani IRO (Akiko Aoki, Yukiko Kajita, Akiko Shigeru, Naoko Sakakura, Mao Hatta, Yukari Kajiwara)
Sample Making Assistants: Satomi Urayama & Taeko Masuya
Proofreader: Masako Mukai
Interview Text: Noriko Tanaka
Pattern Grading: Kazuhiro Ueno
Tracing: Fumiko Shirai
Digital Tracing: Akane Uno (Bunka Phototype)
Pattern: Yukiko Kajita
Editors: Noriko Takai & Kaori Tanaka (Bunka Publishing Bureau)
Cooperation: Kokka Co., Ltd.
English Editor: Lindsay Fair
Translation: Ai Jirka

ISBN: 978-1-940552-69-9

Printed in China

10 9 8 7 6 5 4 3 2 1

JAPANESE DRESSMAKERS

A Year *of* Sewing *with* Nani Iro

18 Patterns to Make & Wear
Throughout the Seasons

Naomi Ito

Contents

The Projects

Introduction

The word "nani" means beautiful in Hawaiian, while the word "iro" means colors in Japanese. It's been over 20 years since the textile brand Nani Iro first launched. Inspired by the seasons and the elements of nature, including the colors, movement, and light, I create watercolor paintings that are then converted into textiles. I am so inspired by nature and enjoy creating this art so much that I could continue this work for the rest of my life. Today, Nani Iro fabrics are available in over 30 countries and I am honored that people use my fabrics to create garments that they wear everyday.

Several years ago, we opened the Atelier to Nani Iro in Osaka, Japan to help those interested in using Nani Iro fabric to sew their own clothes. The staff at the atelier is very knowledgeable about the fabric and about garment sewing. One of my favorite things about Nani Iro fabric is that you can create unique impressions by choosing which specific areas of the print you'll use to cut out certain pattern pieces. My desire is that you make your selections based on what feels right to you—I believe this will make your handmade garments even more special.

The 20th anniversary collection of Nani Iro fabric was used for the designs in this book.

We spent over two years developing the patterns for this book. Inspired by the four seasons and by the flow of the day, from sunrise to sunset, we composed a wardrobe story that can be worn all year long. I learned so much from the wonderful atelier staff and loved seeing Nani Iro fabric through their eyes. Each team member has their own individual style and helped me create new combinations and interpretations that would not have been possible on my own.

My hope is that you are inspired by the patterns and outfits included in this book, but that you also feel empowered to add your own modifications and create your own designs. To me, selecting your own fabric and sewing your own clothes is one of the most joyous adventures in life!

—Naomi Ito

"*Start with a small piece of fabric, create a world of abundance*"

Planet
Look up the dawn sky

A | Cocoon Blouse

J | Wide Leg Pants

Spring mist turns into light and fills the window

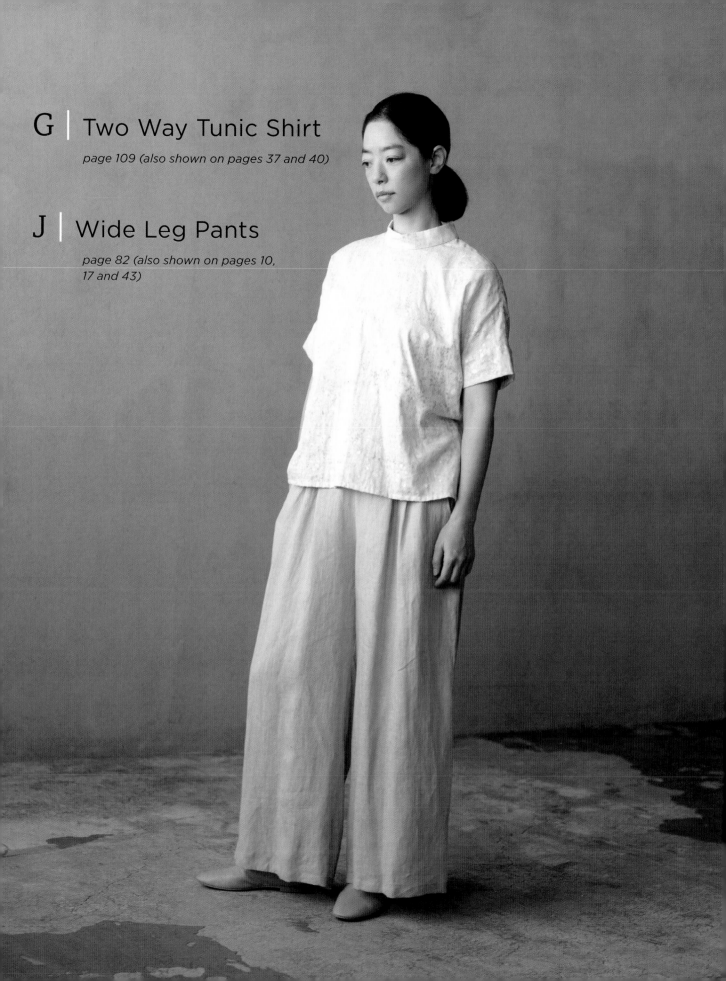

G | Two Way Tunic Shirt

page 109 (also shown on pages 37 and 40)

J | Wide Leg Pants

page 82 (also shown on pages 10, 17 and 43)

The world is fascinated by the moment
Like after the rain

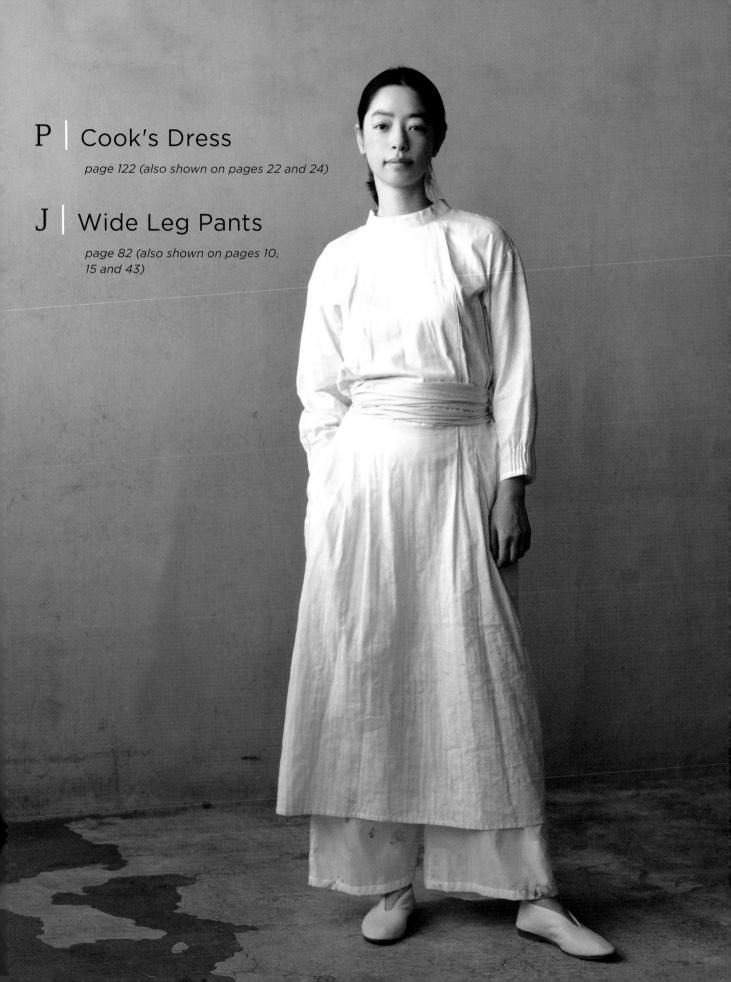

P | Cook's Dress

J | Wide Leg Pants

Melting scenery of calm spring

A | Cocoon Blouse

page 66 (also shown on pages 10 and 30)

F | Stand Collar Dress

*page 102 (also shown on pages 21
and 34)*

On the way home after picking violets
Beautiful things you saw as a child

P | Cook's Dress

page 122 (also shown on pages 17 and 24)

P | Cook's Dress

page 122 (also shown on pages 17 and 22)

Lei nani
Send a wreath

C | Bias Tank Top

page 72 (also shown on page 29)

L | Wrap Front Pants

page 90 (also shown on pages 13, 28 and 40)

Paradise
Oasis like music

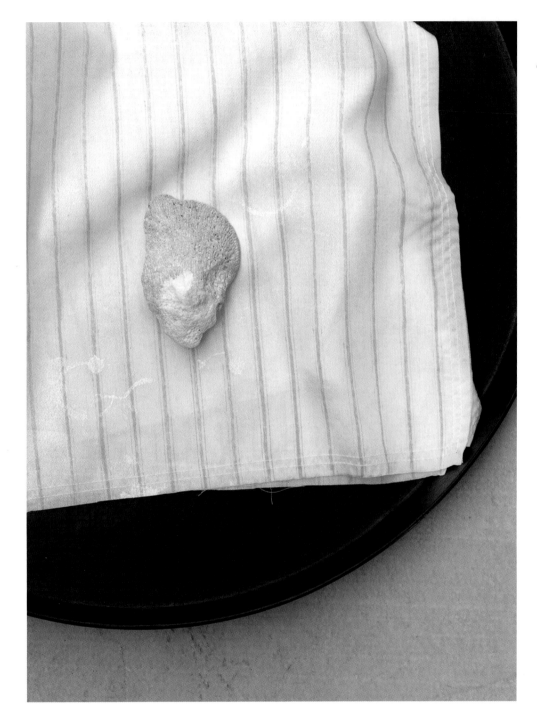

H | Two Way Tunic Dress

page 109

K | Farmer's Pants

page 82 (also shown on page 37)

E | Freedom Tank

page 79 (also shown on page 44)

L | Wrap Front Pants

page 90 (also shown on pages 13, 25 and 40)

D | Cocoon Vest

page 76 (also shown on page 41)

C | Bias Tank Top

page 72 (also shown on page 25)

M | Antique Skirt

page 92 (also shown on pages 30 and 45)

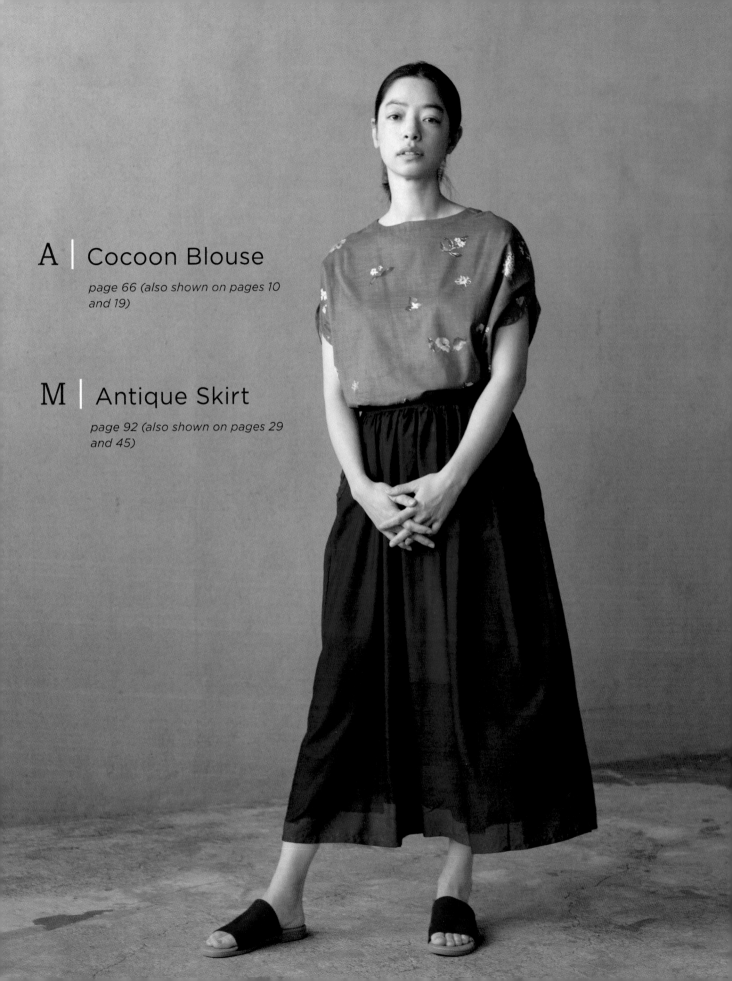

A | Cocoon Blouse

page 66 (also shown on pages 10 and 19)

M | Antique Skirt

page 92 (also shown on pages 29 and 45)

Q | Short Sleeve Gathered Dress

page 128

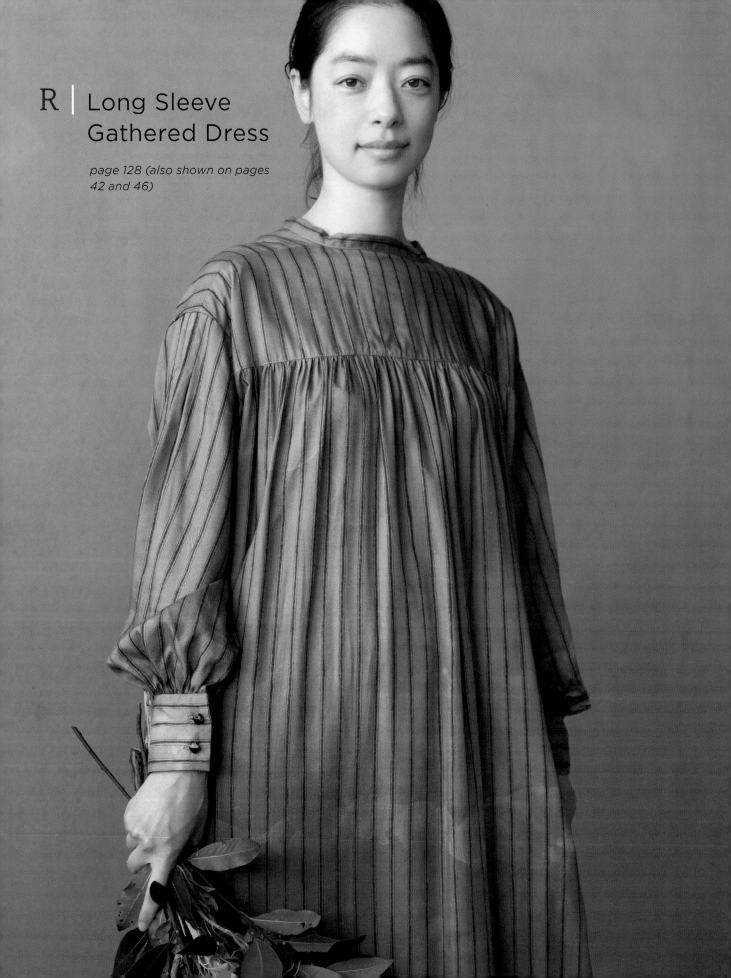

R | Long Sleeve
Gathered Dress

*page 128 (also shown on pages
42 and 46)*

F | Stand Collar Dress

page 102 (also shown on pages 20 and 21)

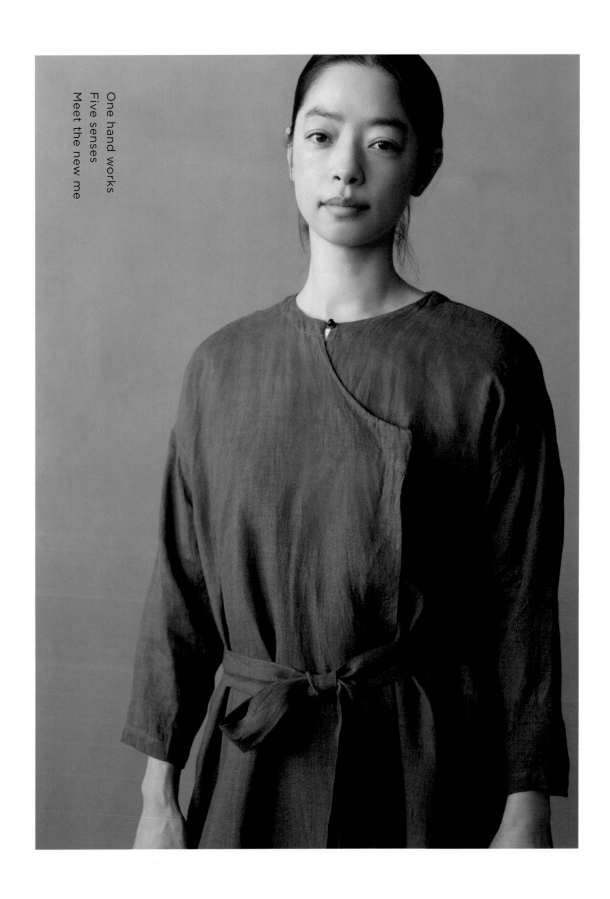

One hand works
Five senses
Meet the new me

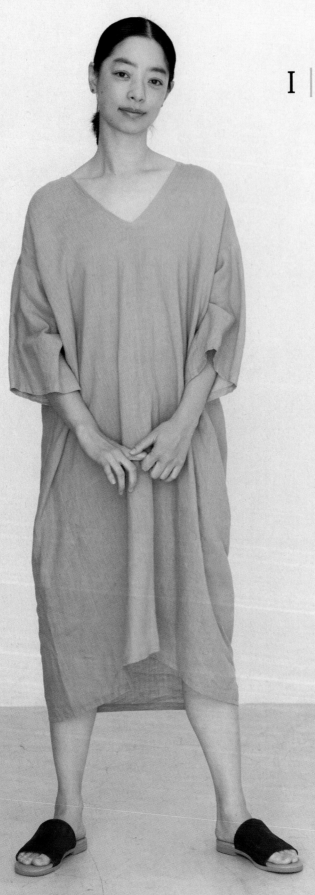

I | V-Neck Tunic

page 96 (also shown on pages 39 and 41)

At dusk on a cherished day

G | Two Way Tunic Shirt

page 109 (also shown on pages 14 and 37)

L | Wrap Front Pants

page 90 (shown on pages 13, 25 and 28)

D | Cocoon Vest

page 76 (also shown on page 29)

I | V-Neck Tunic

page 96 (also shown on pages 38 and 39)

B | Felted Cocoon Dress

page 69 (also shown on page 43)

R | Long Sleeve
Gathered Dress

page 128 (also shown on pages 32 and 46)

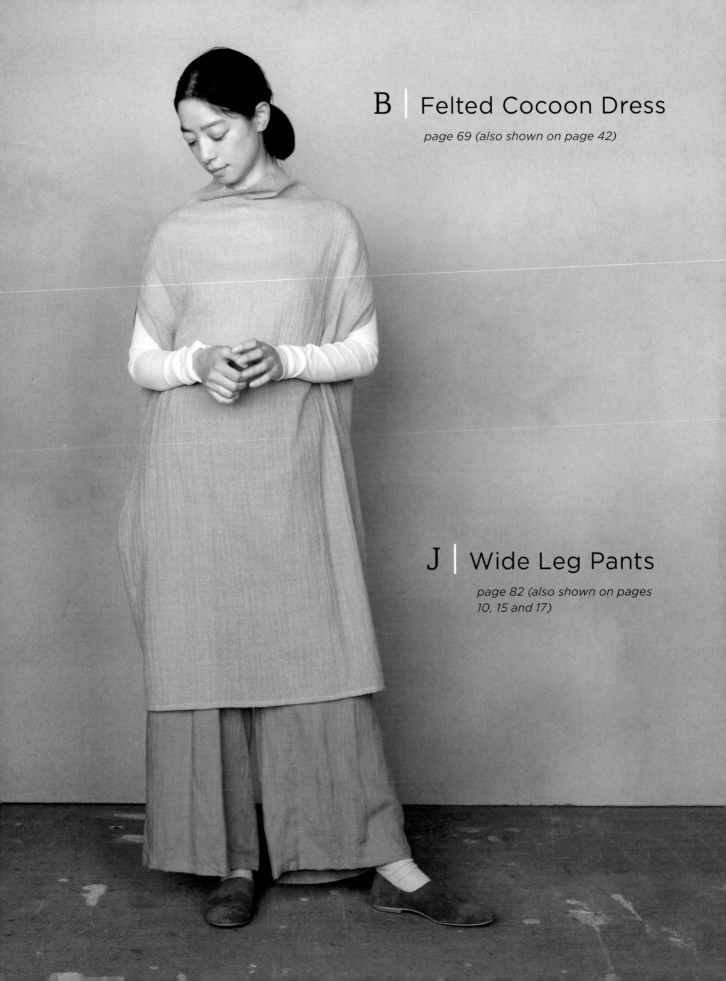

B | Felted Cocoon Dress

page 69 (also shown on page 42)

J | Wide Leg Pants

page 82 (also shown on pages 10, 15 and 17)

E | Freedom Tank

M | Antique Skirt

R | Long Sleeve
Gathered Dress

*page 128 (also shown on pages 32
and 42)*

Fruit that pours light
To a vessel,
To a small boat,
To a piece of cloth

Model: Miwako Ichikawa | Photographer: Jun Okada | Stylist: Setsuko Todoroki | Hair & Make-Up: Hiromi Chinone | Graphic Designer: Kei Sumiya | Textiles & Words: Naomi Ito | Sewing: ATELIER to nani IRO

Around the end of winter light,
Spring has come
Later, summer and fall
I'm still in love

Remembering things that
once made you happy
Makes you feel happy
once again

The Fabric

The fabric throughout this book is the 20th anniversary collection of Nani Iro. This line of fabrics is developed directly from Naomi Ito's original watercolor artwork. Inspired by nature, these fabrics are known for their vibrant colors and poetic movement.

Spring

page 17

Hakko
Cotton silk

page 10

A | Cocoon Blouse

After the Rain
Cotton double gauze

pages 10 and 15

J | Wide Leg Pants

Flax Beige
Linen

page 13

N | Cache-Coeur Short Sleeve Dress & L | Wrap Front Pants

Antique White
Linen

page 14

L | Two Way Tunic Shirt

Birds Eye
Cotton double gauze

Summer

page 22

P | Cook's Dress

New Morning
Cotton silk

page 24

P | Cook's Dress

Lei Nani
Linen

page 25

C | Bias Tank Top & L | Wrap Front Pants

Fuccra: Rakuen
Linen

page 26

Piece by Piece
Lyocell

page 27

H | Two Way Tunic Dress

Piece by Piece
Lyocell

page 27

K | Farmer's Pants

Cinnamon Red
Linen

Autumn

page 31

Q | Sleeveless Gathered Dress

Peacock Green
Linen

page 32

R | Long Sleeve Gathered Dress

Piece by Piece
Lyocell

page 34

F | Stand Collar Dress

Cinnamon Red
Linen

page 36

O | Cache-Cœur Coat

Smokey Grape
Linen

page 37

O | Cache-Cœur Coat

Air Time
Cotton linen

Winter

page 40

G | Two Way Tunic Shirt

New Morning
Cotton silk

page 40

L | Wrap Front Pants

Ash Beige
Linen

page 41

D | Cocoon Vest

Faux Fur
Organic cotton

page 41

I | V-Neck Tunic

Prism Yellow
Linen

page 42

B | Felted Cocoon Dress

Wool gauze

Included below is a visual guide to the fabric used for the designs in this book. The fabrics are organized by season, but you can mix and match to create a versatile, year-round wardrobe.

page 16

P | Cook's Dress

After the Rain
Cotton double gauze

page 17

J | Wide Leg Pants

New Morning
Cotton silk

page 19

A | Cocoon Blouse

Air Time
Cotton double gauze

page 20

F | Stand Collar Dress

New Morning
Cotton double gauze

page 21

Air Time
Cotton linen

page 21

Fuwari Fuwari
Cotton double gauze

page 28

E | Freedom Tank

New Morning
Cotton silk

page 28

L | Wrap Front Pants

Bougainvillea
Linen

page 29

D | Cocoon Vest & M | Antique Skirt

Clear Black
Linen

page 29

C | Bias Tank Top

New Morning
Cotton linen

page 30

A | Cocoon Blouse

New Morning
Cotton linen

page 30

M | Antique Skirt

Wild Flower
Lyocell

page 37

G | Two Way Tunic Shirt

Piece by Piece
Linen

page 37

K | Farmer's Pants

Hakko
Linen

page 38

I | V-Neck Tunic

Ash Beige
Linen

page 39

I | V-Neck Tunic

Hakko
Cotton silk

page 43

B | Felted Cocoon Dress

Wool gauze

page 43

J | Wide Leg Pants

Taupe
Linen

page 44

E | Freedom Tank

Ice Gray
Linen

page 44

M | Antique Skirt

Piece by Piece
Lyocell

pages 42 and 46

R | Long Sleeve Gathered Dress

Hakko
Linen

Exploring the Garment Designs

In this section, we'll take a closer look at the garment designs and explore fabric selections and styling suggestions. Each pattern is ranked by difficulty level according to the following scale.

DIFFICULTY LEVEL

✄ Beginner-friendly project that can be finished in one day

✄ ✄ Confident beginner

✄ ✄ ✄ Intermediate

✄ ✄ ✄ ✄ More difficult

✄ ✄ ✄ ✄ ✄ Challenging

A | Cocoon Blouse ✄

This top features a rounded silhouette with a longer back hemline for elongated movement. Because the design includes side slits, you can wear the blouse partially tucked in for a relaxed, casual look or dress it up for a more elegant ensemble.

page 19
Air Time
Cotton double gauze

page 10
After the Rain
Cotton double gauze

page 30
New Morning
Cotton silk

B | Felted Cocoon Dress ✄

When stitched up in a wool fabric, this dress makes for a warm winter layer that can be felted for added texture and coziness. This simple design is made with just one pattern piece and looks great worn as a dress or layered over a skirt or pants.

page 43
Wool gauze

page 42
Wool gauze

C | Bias Tank Top ✄

Finish the neckline and armholes with coordinating bias tape to elevate a basic tank top. Pair the tank with matching pants to create a jumpsuit-inspired look or make several in your favorite fabrics to have on hand for layering.

page 29
New Morning
Cotton silk

page 25
Fuccra: Rakuen
Linen

D | Cocoon Vest

This artsy vest can be made in lightweight linen for the summer or cozy faux fur for the winter. It makes for a stylish topper for dresses or long sleeve shirts.

page 41

Organic cotton
faux fur

page 29

Clear Black
Linen

E | Freedom Tank

Use the drawstring ties to adjust the gathers and experiment with the silhouette on this unique sleeveless tunic. You can even lengthen the hemline to make a dress version of this design, as shown on page 61.

page 28

New Morning
Cotton silk

page 44

Ice Gray
Linen

F | Stand Collar Dress

This elegant dress features waistline tucks for a more fitted silhouette and a high collar. Other than the neckline, it's made with predominantly straight seams.

page 20

New Morning
Cotton double gauze

Back view

page 21

Fuwari Fuwari
Cotton double
gauze

page 34

Cinnamon Red
Linen

page 21

Air Time
Cotton linen

G | Two Way Tunic Shirt ✂✂✂

This design is reversible—wear with the buttons in the front for a henley-style blouse or with the buttons in the back for a dressier, high neck blouse.

H | Two Way Tunic Dress ✂✂✂

Extend the length of the Two Way Tunic Shirt to create this easy, breezy dress. The pattern features deep side slits, making it easy to walk and move when wearing this dress.

page 37
Piece by Piece
Linen

Back view

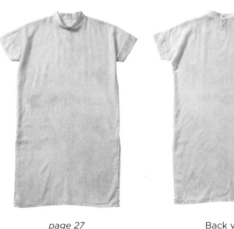

page 27
Piece by Piece
Lyocell

Back view

page 14
Birds Eye
Cotton double gauze

page 40
New Morning
Cotton silk

I | V-Neck Tunic ✂✂✂

This sophisticated dress can be worn with the radiating neckline darts in the front or with the v-neck in front for a simple, yet elegant look.

page 41
Prism Yellow
Linen

Back view

page 38
Ash Beige
Linen

page 39
Hakko
Cotton silk

J | Wide Leg Pants ✂ ✂ ✂

These wide leg pants offer the elegant look of a skirt, but provide the comfort and flexibility of pants. The front waistband creates a polished look when paired with tucked in blouses.

pages 10 and 15
Flax Beige
Linen

page 17
New Morning
Cotton silk

page 43
Taupe
Linen

K | Farmer's Pants ✂ ✂ ✂

Made from the same pattern as the Wide Leg Pants, this design has a cropped, rounded hemline made with darts. This detail allows for movement and comfort, while still providing a tapered silhouette.

page 27
Cinnamon Red
Linen

page 37
Hakko
Linen

L | Wrap Front Pants ✂ ✂ ✂

A simple fold creates an artistic, modern silhouette that can be dressed up or down. Pair these unique pants with cropped or tucked in blouses to show off the beautiful waist detailing. These pants feature an elastic waistband and are cut loose through the hips, then taper in at the ankles.

page 13
Antique White
Linen

page 25
Fuccra: Rakuen
Linen

page 28
Bougainvillea
Linen

page 40
Ash Beige
Linen

M | Antique Skirt ✂✂✂

This simple skirt design was inspired by historical clothing. The gathers are positioned high to flatter the hips and the hemline is a little longer for an elegant look.

page 45
Piece by Piece
Lyocell

page 30
Wild Flower
Lyocell

page 29
Clear Black
Linen

N | Cache-Cœur Short Sleeve Dress

✂✂✂✂

French for "hide the heart," cache-cœur tops and dresses utilize overlapping fronts to create a wrap effect. This structured dress can be worn belted or loose. It includes a secret inner button for a clean, minimalist look.

page 13
Antique White
Linen

O | Cache-Cœur Coat ✂✂✂✂

Add sleeves to the Cache-Cœur Short Sleeve Dress for a versatile piece that can be worn as a dress or coat.

page 36
Smokey Grape
Linen

Back view

page 37
Air Time
Cotton linen

P | Cook's Dress ✂✂✂✂✂

Inspired by a chef's coat, this dress features many special details, including a fitted waistband with gathers and tucks along the sleeve cuffs.

page 22
New Morning
Cotton silk

Back view

page 17
After the Rain
Cotton double gauze

page 24
Lei Nani
Linen

Q | Short Sleeve Gathered Dress ✂✂✂✂

This sleeveless dress is perfect for summer, especially when made from linen or cotton double gauze. It features a pretty tie collar than can be worn loose or in a bow.

page 31
Peacock Green
Linen

R | Long Sleeve Gathered Dress ✂✂✂✂✂

This dress uses gathers just about everywhere—around the sleeve caps, cuffs, and yokes. Opt for fabrics that are easy to manipulate, such as cotton silk or lyocell. This design features an elegantly finished yoke, so it's geared toward more advanced sewists.

page 32
Piece by Piece
Lyocell

Back view

page 46
Hakko
Linen

Experimenting with the Patterns

The patterns included in this book were created as a collaborative effort by the atelier staff. The team spent two years gathering ideas, constructing samples, and refining the designs to stand up to everyday life. One of the most amazing byproducts of this process was seing all the unique interpretations of the patterns—each as original as its maker. We've included some of our favorite ideas for modifying and personalizing the patterns from the book and encourage you to experiment with your own ideas.

CHANGE THE FABRIC

Main fabric: New Morning cotton silk
Accent fabric: Bougainvillea linen

Q | Short Sleeve Gathered Dress
As a blouse with contrasting collar

Instructions on page 128

Simply shorten the length by 20" (50 cm) to transform the dress into a blouse. Here, solid fuchsia accent fabric was used for the tie collar and placket to create a striking look.

Size shown: Medium
Main fabric: 3 ¼ yds (2.9 m) of 41" (104 cm) wide fabric
Accent fabric: 1 ½ yds (1.4 m) of 41" (104 cm) wide fabric

M | Antique Skirt
With contrasting plackets

Instructions on page 92

Use a solid contrast fabric for the pocket plackets to really make this detail stand out. You can even coordinate it with the accent fabric used on the blouse for a matching set.

Size shown: Medium
Main fabric: 2 ½ yds (2.2 m) of 41" (104 cm) wide fabric
Accent fabric: 8" x 8" (20 × 20 cm)

ADD SPECIAL DETAILS

I | V-Neck Tunic
Add hand embroidery

Instructions on page 96

Use hand stitching to accentuate the radiating lines created by the neckline darts. Use matching thread for a subtle look or opt for a contrasting color to create a bold effect.

Fabric: Prism Yellow linen

C | Bias Tank Top
Add gathers

Instructions on page 72

Alter the silhouette by adding gathers along the side seams. Follow the instructions to complete the tank top, add gathering stitches to the seam allowance, pull the thread tails until you create the desired amount of ruching and secure in place. These tank tops are ideal for layering, allowing you to experiment with color combinations. You can also lengthen the hemline to transform the tank top into a tunic.

Fabric: Prism Yellow linen

CHANGE THE LENGTH

A | Cocoon Blouse
Lengthen the hemline

Instructions on page 66

Left: The Cocoon Blouse made following the pattern, which features a longer back hemline.

Right: The Cocoon Blouse made with an extended front hemline so the front matches the back.

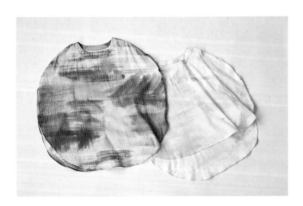

Extend the hemline of the front to match that of the back. Lengthening the hemline creates a more rounded, cocoon silhouette that looks great with a pair of pants.

Fabric: Air Time double gauze
Size shown: Medium
Yardage: 2 yds (1.7 m) of 41" (104 cm) wide fabric

F | Stand Collar Dress
As a tunic

Instructions on page 102

For those with a petite stature, try shortening any of the dress patterns into a knee-length tunic. Tunics look great paired with the Farmer's Pants (see page 82).

Fabric: Lei Nani linen
Size shown: Small
Yardage: 2 ½ yds (2 m) of 41" (104 cm) wide fabric

E | Freedom Tank
As a dress

Instructions on page 79

P | Cook's Dress
As a blouse

Instructions on page 122

Omit the skirt to convert the dress into a blouse. On step 7, fold the bottom ⅜" (1 cm) of both the inside and outside waistbands under and stitch in place to create the hem.

Fabric: Mist Rose linen (left) and Taupe linen (right)
Size shown: Medium
Yardage: 2 ¼ yds (1.9 m) of 41" (104 cm) wide fabric

Add 24" (60 cm) to the length to transform the Freedom Tank into a long dress. You can create different impressions depending on how you tie the drawstrings—pull them tight for a blousy effect with a fitted waist, or leave them loose for a more casual look.

Fabric: Piece by Piece linen
Yardage: 3 ½ yds (3.1 m) of 41" (104 cm) wide fabric

N | Cache-Cœur Short Sleeve Dress

As a bolero

Instructions on page 116

O | Cache-Cœur Coat

Shorten the length

Instructions on page 116

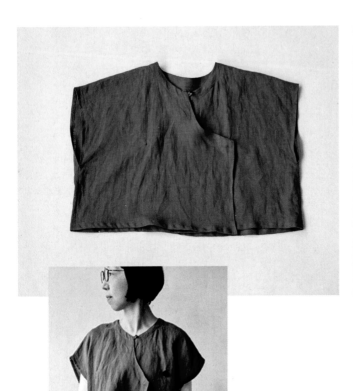

Here, the dress was shortened 26 ½" (67 cm) to make a bolero jacket. Without a belt or pockets, this lightweight layer has a casual, airy feel.

Fabric: Amish Blue linen
Size shown: Medium
Yardage: 1 ½ yds (1.4 m) of 41" (104 cm) wide fabric

Shorten the length by 15 ¾" (40 cm) for a cute jacket that can be word belted or open.

Fabric: Wild Flower lyocell
Size shown: Medium
Yardage: 3 yds (2.8 m) of 41" (104 cm) wide fabric

D | Cocoon Vest
Reversible patchwork

Instructions on page 76

Create a one-of-a-kind piece by constructing your own collage-style fabric using scraps. Appliqué the scraps to your main fabric, arranging them as your heart desires, and embellish with hand or machine embroidery. Next, cut the pattern pieces out of this handmade fabric and construct the garment. The sample shown here includes a lining and is actually reversible.

Size shown: Medium
Main fabric: 3 yds (2.8 m) of 41" (104 cm) wide fabric
Scraps: Assorted sizes

Lining fabric: Wild Flower lyocell

Before You Begin

SELECTING YOUR SIZE

The patterns included in this book range in size from S-XL, though the relaxed style of many of the garments will fit a more inclusive size range.

Use the chart included below to help determine which garment size to make based on your body measurements. Note: You may need to adjust the length to suit your height.

	S	M	L	XL
Bust	32"-34 ½" (81.5-87.5 cm)	34"-36 ½" (86.5-92.5 cm)	36"-40 ½" (91.5-103 cm)	40"-43" (101.5-109 cm)
Waist	24"-27" (61-68.5 cm)	26"-29" (66-73.5 cm)	28"-33" (71-84 cm)	32"-35" (81.5-89 cm)
Hips	34"-37" (86.5-94 cm)	36"-39" (91.5-99 cm)	38"-43" (96.5-109 cm)	42"-45" (106.5-114.5 cm)
Height	59"-60 ¾" (150-154 cm)	61"-65 ½" (155-166 cm)	61"-67" (155-170 cm)	61"-67" (155-170 cm)

Finished size measurements are also included for each project. These dimensions reflect the amount of ease included in the design of the garment. Ease is the difference between the finished garment measurements and your actual body measurements.

Due to the oversized design of many of the garments, we recommend sizing down if you are between sizes.

USING THE PATTERNS

Full-size patterns are included for all of the designs in this book. Begin by locating all of the pattern pieces necessary for the project. Use a highlighter to outline your size on each piece. Make sure to outline all corresponding marks, such as grainline, alignment marks, and facing and pocket placements. Next, transfer the pattern pieces onto a separate sheet of paper, such as tracing paper.

PREPARE YOUR FABRIC

Pre-wash your fabric before cutting and sewing in order to prevent your finished project from shrinking during regular washing.

CUTTING YOUR FABRIC

Each project includes a layout diagram suggesting how to arrange the pattern pieces on the fabric. Use this diagram as a guide, but keep in mind that you may need to arrange your pieces differently based on size or fabric selection. The layouts in this book are based on 41" (104 cm) wide Nani Iro fabrics, which are narrower than the standard 42"-44" (106.5-112 cm) fabric width, so you may need to adjust accordingly. Many of the layout diagrams will call for the fabric to be folded in half with the right sides together and for pattern pieces to be aligned with the fold.

Seam allowance is not included in the patterns so it will need to be added. Refer to the layout diagram for the individual project to determine the amount of seam allowance to add for each pattern piece. In this book, the seam allowance is $\frac{3}{8}$" (1 cm), unless otherwise noted. Use a ruler and chalk to mark the seam allowance around each pattern piece, then cut out the fabric. If the layout diagram shows a 0, do not add seam allowance to that area.

Patterns are not included for certain straight edge pieces, such as drawstrings and bias strips. Use a ruler to measure and mark these pieces directly on the fabric according to the dimensions provided in the project instructions.

BEFORE SEWING

There are a few more steps to take before you get started sewing. These will help ensure a beautifully finished garment. First, you'll need to apply fusible interfacing to certain areas of the garment that will receive a lot of wear and tear, such as cuffs and collars. You'll find these areas noted in the layout diagram. Use light- to medium-weight interfacing for double gauze cottons and linen fabric. And finally, you'll need to finish the raw edges of certain pattern pieces with an overlock machine. If you don't have an overlock machine, use the zigzag stitch on your regular machine instead. The edges that will need to be finished prior to sewing the garment together are noted in the layout diagram for each project.

A | Cocoon Blouse

Shown on pages 10, 19 and 30

Finished Sizes

	S	M	L	XL
Bust	53 ½" (136 cm)	55" (140 cm)	56 ¾" (144 cm)	58 ¾" (149 cm)
Length	28" (71 cm)	28 ¼" (72 cm)	28 ¾" (73.2 cm)	29 ¾" (74.5 cm)

Materials

- 41" (104 cm) wide cotton double gauze or cotton silk (see chart below for yardage)
- 6" x 28" (15 x 70 cm) of fusible interfacing

	S	M	L	XL
Fabric Requirements	1 ¾ yds (1.6 m)	1 ¾ yds (1.6 m)	1 ¾ yds (1.6 m)	2 yds (1.7 m)

Pattern Pieces on Sheet 1

- ☐ Front
- ☐ Back
- ☐ Front facing
- ☐ Back facing

Pattern Layout

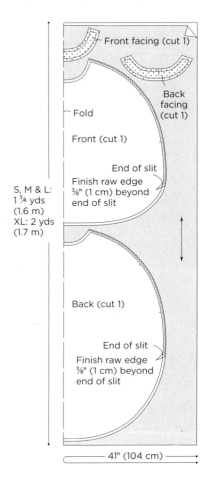

Front facing (cut 1)

Back facing (cut 1)

Fold

Front (cut 1)

End of slit
Finish raw edge ⅜" (1 cm) beyond end of slit

S, M & L: 1 ¾ yds (1.6 m)
XL: 2 yds (1.7 m)

Back (cut 1)

End of slit
Finish raw edge ⅜" (1 cm) beyond end of slit

41" (104 cm)

- Add ⅜" (1 cm) seam allowance, unless otherwise noted.
- Use an overlock machine to finish the raw edges of the front and back, as shown in the above diagram.
- Cut out and adhere fusible interfacing to the wrong side of the fabric for the areas shaded with [⣿⣿].

Construction Steps

1 Sew the side seams, leaving openings for the sleeves (see diagram below).

2 Finish the sleeve openings (see diagram below).

3 Sew the facings together (see page 68).

4 Finish the neckline (see page 68).

5 Hem the bottom (see page 68).

Sew using ⅜" (1 cm) seam allowance, unless otherwise noted.

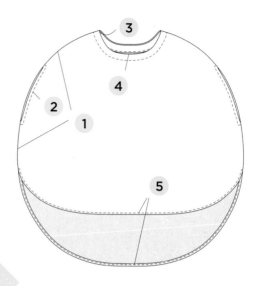

---

1 Sew the side seams, leaving openings for the sleeves

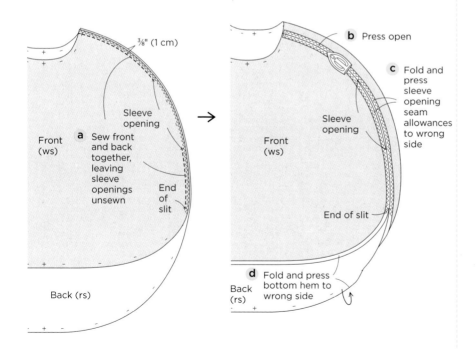

⅜" (1 cm)

Sleeve opening

Front (ws)

a Sew front and back together, leaving sleeve openings unsewn

End of slit

Back (rs)

b Press open

c Fold and press sleeve opening seam allowances to wrong side

Sleeve opening

Front (ws)

End of slit

Back (rs)

d Fold and press bottom hem to wrong side

Note: The bottom hem should be folded over ¼" (5 mm) twice.

2 Finish the sleeve openings

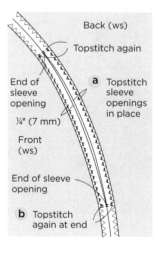

Back (ws)

Topstitch again

End of sleeve opening

¼" (7 mm)

Front (ws)

End of sleeve opening

a Topstitch sleeve openings in place

b Topstitch again at end

3 Sew the facings together

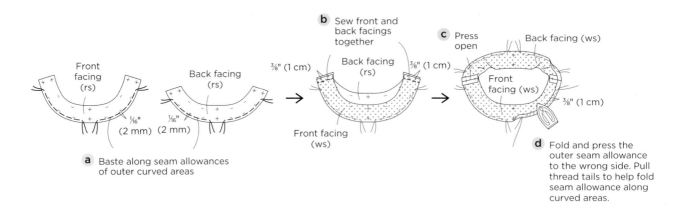

Front facing (rs)

Back facing (rs)

⅟₁₆" (2 mm)   ⅟₁₆" (2 mm)

a Baste along seam allowances of outer curved areas

⅜" (1 cm)   Back facing (rs)   ⅜" (1 cm)

b Sew front and back facings together

Front facing (ws)

c Press open

Back facing (ws)

Front facing (ws)

⅜" (1 cm)

d Fold and press the outer seam allowance to the wrong side. Pull thread tails to help fold seam allowance along curved areas.

---

4 Finish the neckline

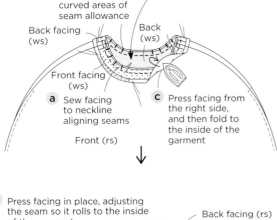

b Make clips into curved areas of seam allowance   ⅜" (1 cm)

Back facing (ws)   Back (ws)

Front facing (ws)

a Sew facing to neckline aligning seams

c Press facing from the right side, and then fold to the inside of the garment

Front (rs)

d Press facing in place, adjusting the seam so it rolls to the inside of the garment

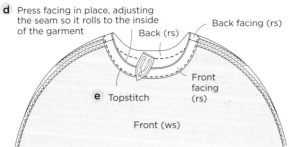

Back (rs)   Back facing (rs)

Front facing (rs)

e Topstitch

Front (ws)

---

5 Hem the bottom

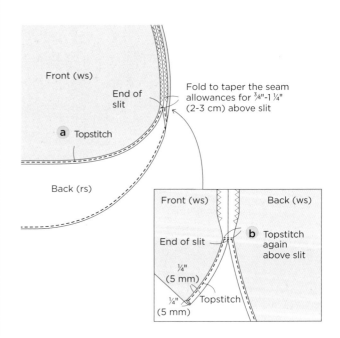

Front (ws)

End of slit

Back (rs)

a Topstitch

Fold to taper the seam allowances for ¾"-1 ¼" (2-3 cm) above slit

Front (ws)   Back (ws)

End of slit

b Topstitch again above slit

¼" (5 mm)

¼" (5 mm)   Topstitch

B | Felted Cocoon Dress

Shown on pages 42 and 43

Finished Sizes

	S	M	L	XL
Bust	55" (140 cm)	57 ½" (146 cm)	59" (150 cm)	61 ½" (156 cm)
Length	43 ¾" (111 cm)	44 ½" (113 cm)	45 ¼" (115 cm)	46" (117 cm)

Materials

- 52" (130 cm) wide wool gauze (see chart below for yardage)

	S	M	L	XL
Fabric Requirements	2 ¾ yds (2.4 m)	2 ¾ yds (2.4 m)	2 ¾ yds (2.5 m)	2 ¾ yds (2.5 m)

Pattern Pieces on Sheet 2

☐ Front & Back*

*Note that the front and back is divided into two pieces in order to fit on the pattern sheet, and will need to be taped together for the complete pattern.

- Add ⅜" (1 cm) seam allowance, unless otherwise noted.
- Do not add seam allowance to areas marked 0.

Pattern Layout

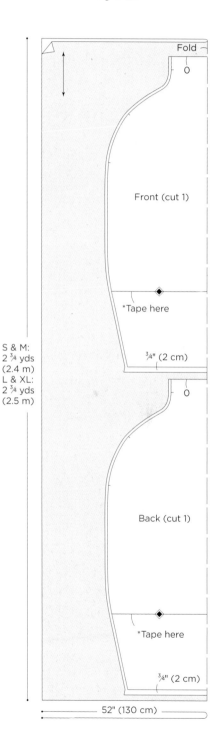

Fold

0

Front (cut 1)

*Tape here

S & M:
2 ¾ yds
(2.4 m)
L & XL:
2 ¾ yds
(2.5 m)

¾" (2 cm)

0

Back (cut 1)

*Tape here

¾" (2 cm)

52" (130 cm)

Construction Steps

1 Sew the side seams, leaving openings for the sleeves (see diagram below).

2 Finish the sleeve openings (see diagram below).

3 Hem the bottom (see page 71).

4 Wash and felt the fabric (see page 71).

Sew using ⅜" (1 cm) seam allowance, unless otherwise noted.

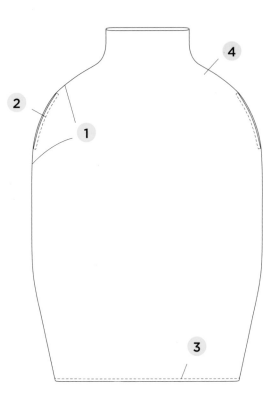

---

1 Sew the side seams, leaving openings for the sleeves

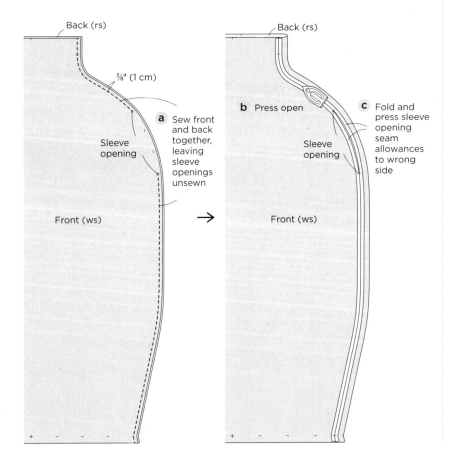

Back (rs)

⅜" (1 cm)

a Sew front and back together, leaving sleeve openings unsewn

Sleeve opening

Front (ws)

Back (rs)

b Press open

c Fold and press sleeve opening seam allowances to wrong side

Sleeve opening

Front (ws)

2 Finish the sleeve openings

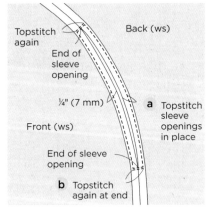

Topstitch again

Back (ws)

End of sleeve opening

¼" (7 mm)

Front (ws)

a Topstitch sleeve openings in place

End of sleeve opening

b Topstitch again at end

3 Hem the bottom

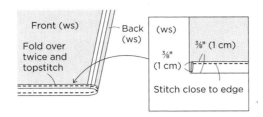

4 Wash and felt the fabric

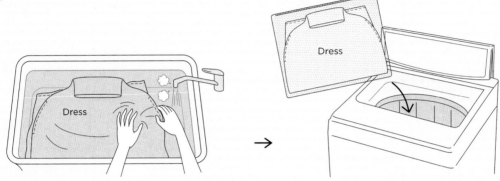

a Soak the dress in hot water (about 104° F [40° C]). Use your hands to agitate the dress for about a minute. Pay extra attention to the seam allowances along the sleeve openings and neck as those are areas that are likely to fray. Felting the fabric in these areas will prevent the seam allowances from unraveling.

b Put the dress in a mesh laundry bag and wash it on the longest agitation setting available on your machine. Remove from the machine and trim any frayed threads.

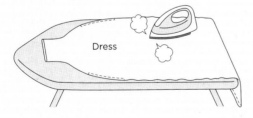

c While the dress is still wet, use a low temperature iron to press the dress into shape, and then let it dry.

Repeat steps a-c until your dress reaches the preferred size and level of felting. Remember, once you shrink the dress, you can't undo it, so felt it a little at a time. If you would like to shrink your dress even more, increase the water temperature, add a bit of laundry detergent, and extend the amount of agitation time.

C | Bias Tank Top

Shown on pages 25 and 29

Finished Sizes

	S	M	L	XL
Bust	37" (94 cm)	39" (99 cm)	40 ½" (103 cm)	43" (109 cm)
Length	28" (70.8 cm)	28 ¼" (71.7 cm)	28 ¾" (72.8 cm)	29 ¼" (74 cm)

Materials

- 41" (104 cm) wide cotton double gauze (see chart below for yardage)

	S	M	L	XL
Fabric Requirements	2 yds (1.8 m)	2 yds (1.8 m)	2 yds (1.8 m)	2 ¼ yds (1.9 m)

Pattern Pieces on Sheet 4

- ☐ Front
- ☐ Back
- ☐ Armhole bias strip
- ☐ Neckline bias strip

- Add ⅜" (1 cm) seam allowance, unless otherwise noted.
- Do not add seam allowance to areas marked 0.
- Use an overlock machine to finish the raw edges of the front and back, as shown in the above diagram.

Pattern Layout

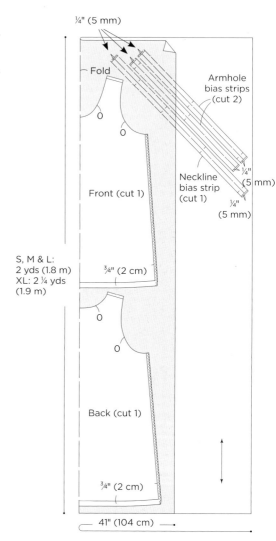

Construction Steps

1. Sew the shoulders (see diagram below).

2. Sew the side seams and make the slits (see page 74).

3. Finish the neckline (see page 74).

4. Finish the armholes (see page 75).

5. Hem the bottom (see page 75).

Sew using ⅜" (1 cm) seam allowance, unless otherwise noted.

---

1 Sew the shoulders

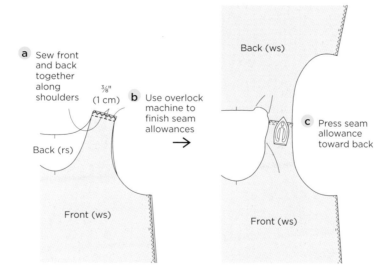

a Sew front and back together along shoulders

⅜" (1 cm)

b Use overlock machine to finish seam allowances →

Back (rs)

Front (ws)

Back (ws)

c Press seam allowance toward back

Front (ws)

2 Sew the side seams and make the slits

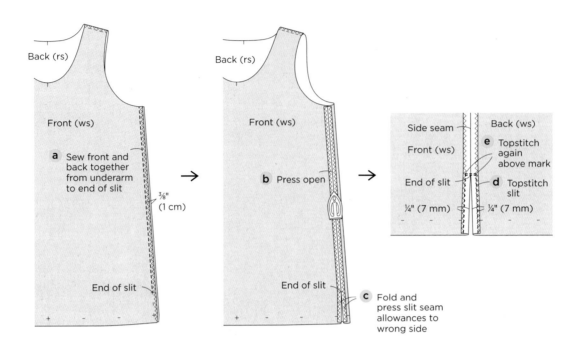

Back (rs)

Front (ws)

a Sew front and back together from underarm to end of slit

⅜" (1 cm)

End of slit

→

Back (rs)

Front (ws)

b Press open

End of slit

c Fold and press slit seam allowances to wrong side

→

Side seam

Front (ws)

End of slit

¼" (7 mm)

Back (ws)

e Topstitch again above mark

d Topstitch slit

¼" (7 mm)

3 Finish the neckline

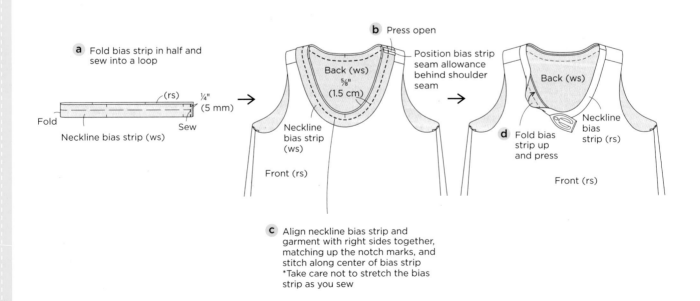

a Fold bias strip in half and sew into a loop

Fold

(rs)

¼" (5 mm)

Sew

Neckline bias strip (ws)

→

b Press open

Position bias strip seam allowance behind shoulder seam

Back (ws)
⅝" (1.5 cm)

Neckline bias strip (ws)

Front (rs)

c Align neckline bias strip and garment with right sides together, matching up the notch marks, and stitch along center of bias strip
*Take care not to stretch the bias strip as you sew

→

Back (ws)

d Fold bias strip up and press

Neckline bias strip (rs)

Front (rs)

4 Finish the armholes

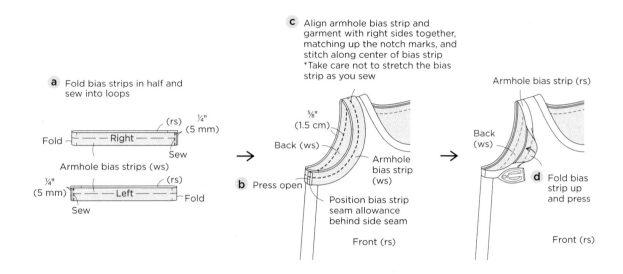

a Fold bias strips in half and sew into loops

Fold — (rs) ¼" (5 mm)
— Right — Sew

Armhole bias strips (ws)

¼" (5 mm) — Left — (rs) Fold
Sew

b Press open

c Align armhole bias strip and garment with right sides together, matching up the notch marks, and stitch along center of bias strip
*Take care not to stretch the bias strip as you sew

⅝" (1.5 cm)
Back (ws)
Armhole bias strip (ws)
Position bias strip seam allowance behind side seam
Front (rs)

Armhole bias strip (rs)
Back (ws)
d Fold bias strip up and press
Front (rs)

5 Hem the bottom

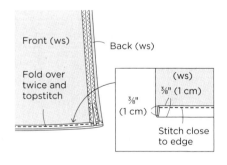

Front (ws)
Back (ws)
Fold over twice and topstitch

(ws)
⅜" (1 cm)
⅜" (1 cm)
Stitch close to edge

D | Cocoon Vest

Shown on pages 29 and 41

Finished Sizes

	S	M	L	XL
Bust	56 ¼" (143 cm)	58 ¼" (148 cm)	59 ¾" (152 cm)	62 ¼" (158 cm)
Length	23" (58.5 cm)	23 ½" (59.5 cm)	24" (60.7 cm)	24 ½" (62 cm)

Materials

- 41" (104 cm) wide linen or organic cotton faux fur (see chart below for yardage)
- 28" x 28" (70 x 70 cm) of fusible interfacing
- One ¾" (2 cm) diameter button

	S	M	L	XL
Fabric Requirements	2 ¼ yds (1.9 m)	2 ¼ yds (1.9 m)	2 ¼ yds (2 m)	2 ¼ yds (2 m)

Pattern Pieces on Sheet 4

- ☐ Front
- ☐ Back
- ☐ Front facing
- ☐ Back facing

Pattern Layout

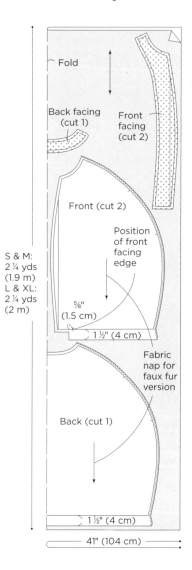

Fold

Back facing (cut 1)

Front facing (cut 2)

Front (cut 2)

Position of front facing edge

S & M: 2 ¼ yds (1.9 m)
L & XL: 2 ¼ yds (2 m)

⅝" (1.5 cm)

1 ½" (4 cm)

Fabric nap for faux fur version

Back (cut 1)

1 ½" (4 cm)

41" (104 cm)

- Add ⅜" (1 cm) seam allowance, unless otherwise noted.
- Use an overlock machine to finish the raw edges of the front and back, as shown in the above diagram.
- Cut out and adhere fusible interfacing to the wrong side of the fabric for the areas shaded with ▦.

Construction Steps

1 Sew the side seams, leaving openings for the sleeves (see diagram below).

2 Finish the sleeve openings (see diagram below).

3 Sew the facings together (see page 78).

4 Attach the facings and hem the bottom (see page 78).

5 Make a buttonhole and attach the button (refer to pattern for placement).

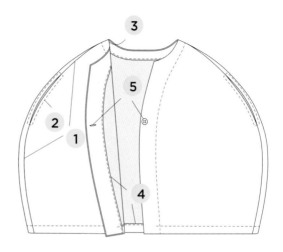

Sew using ⅜" (1 cm) seam allowance, unless otherwise noted.

1 Sew the side seams, leaving openings for the sleeves

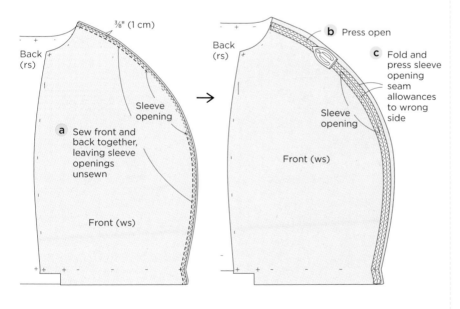

⅜" (1 cm)

Back (rs)

Sleeve opening

a Sew front and back together, leaving sleeve openings unsewn

Front (ws)

Back (rs)

b Press open

c Fold and press sleeve opening seam allowances to wrong side

Sleeve opening

Front (ws)

2 Finish the sleeve openings

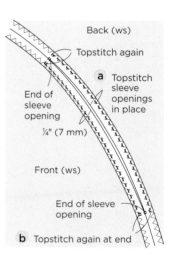

Back (ws)

Topstitch again

a Topstitch sleeve openings in place

End of sleeve opening

¼" (7 mm)

Front (ws)

End of sleeve opening

b Topstitch again at end

3 Sew the facings together

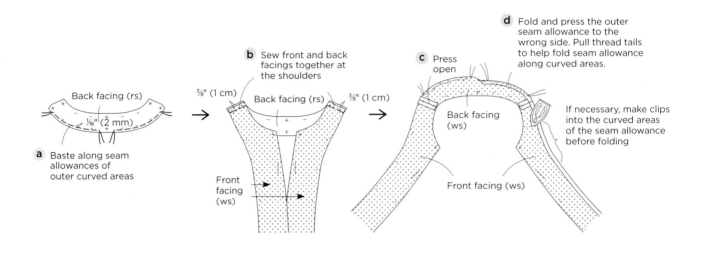

a Baste along seam allowances of outer curved areas

Back facing (rs)

1/16" (2 mm)

b Sew front and back facings together at the shoulders

3/8" (1 cm) Back facing (rs) 3/8" (1 cm)

Front facing (ws)

c Press open

Back facing (ws)

Front facing (ws)

d Fold and press the outer seam allowance to the wrong side. Pull thread tails to help fold seam allowance along curved areas.

If necessary, make clips into the curved areas of the seam allowance before folding

4 Attach the facings and hem the bottom

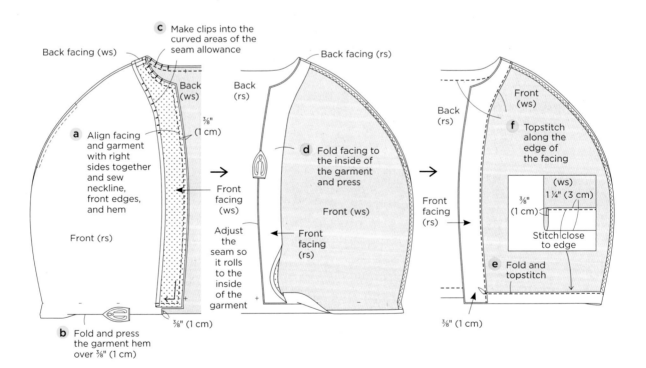

c Make clips into the curved areas of the seam allowance

Back facing (ws)

Back (ws)

Back (rs)

3/8" (1 cm)

a Align facing and garment with right sides together and sew neckline, front edges, and hem

Front (rs)

Front facing (ws)

Adjust the seam so it rolls to the inside of the garment

b Fold and press the garment hem over 3/8" (1 cm)

Back facing (rs)

d Fold facing to the inside of the garment and press

Front (ws)

Front facing (rs)

Front facing (rs)

Back (rs)

Front (ws)

f Topstitch along the edge of the facing

(ws) 1 1/4" (3 cm)

3/8" (1 cm)

Stitch close to edge

e Fold and topstitch

3/8" (1 cm)

3/8" (1 cm)

E | Freedom Tank

Shown on pages 28 and 44

Finished Size

	O/S
Bust	45 ¼" (115 cm)
Length	29" (74 cm)

Materials

- 2 ¼ yds (1.9 m) of 41" (104 cm) wide cotton silk or linen
- 19 ¾" x 6" (50 x 15 cm) of fusible interfacing
- Two ⅜" (1 cm) diameter button

Pattern Pieces on Sheet 1

- ☐ Front
- ☐ Back
- ☐ Front facing
- ☐ Back facing

There are no pattern pieces for the button loop or drawstring. Cut following the dimensions listed below:

- ☐ Button loop (cut 1 on the bias): ¾" x 5 ⅛" (1.8 x 13 cm)
- ☐ Drawstring (cut 2): 1 ½" x 56" (4 x 142 cm)

Pattern Layout

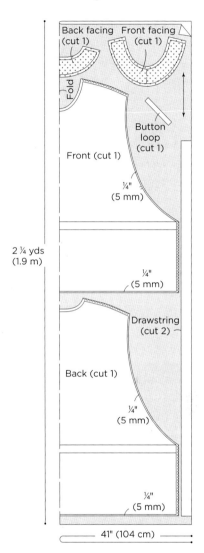

- Add ⅜" (1 cm) seam allowance, unless otherwise noted.
- Use an overlock machine to finish the raw edges of the front and back, as shown in the above diagram.
- Cut out and adhere fusible interfacing to the wrong side of the fabric for the areas shaded with ▨.

Construction Steps

1　Sew the shoulders (see diagram below).

2　Sew the facings together (see step 3 on page 68).

3　Finish the neckline (see step 4 on page 68).

4　Sew the side seams (see diagram below).

5　Make the drawstring casing (see page 81).

6　Make the button loops and attach to the front, then attach the buttons to the back (see page 81).

7　Make the drawstring and insert through casing (see page 81).

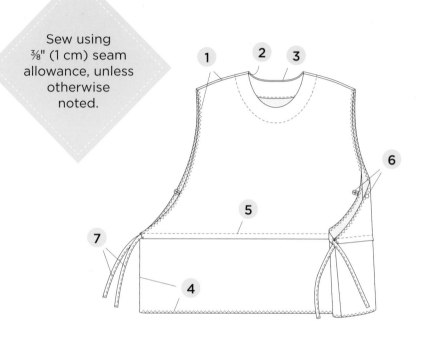

Sew using ⅜" (1 cm) seam allowance, unless otherwise noted.

1　Sew the shoulders

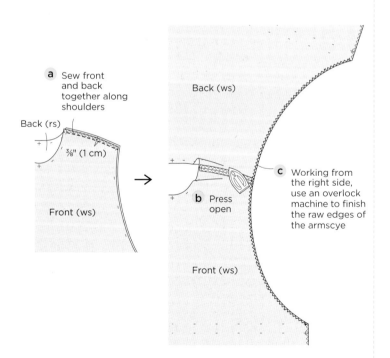

a Sew front and back together along shoulders

Back (rs)

⅜" (1 cm)

Front (ws)

Back (ws)

b Press open

Front (ws)

c Working from the right side, use an overlock machine to finish the raw edges of the armscye

4　Sew the side seams

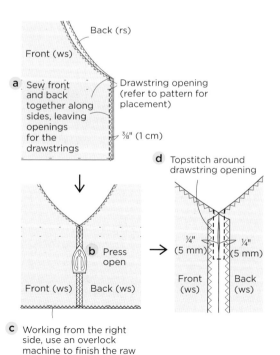

Back (rs)

Front (ws)

a Sew front and back together along sides, leaving openings for the drawstrings

Drawstring opening (refer to pattern for placement)

⅜" (1 cm)

b Press open

Front (ws)　Back (ws)

c Working from the right side, use an overlock machine to finish the raw edges of the hem

d Topstitch around drawstring opening

¼" (5 mm)　¼" (5 mm)

Front (ws)　Back (ws)

5 Make the drawstring casing

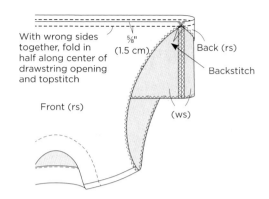

With wrong sides together, fold in half along center of drawstring opening and topstitch

⅝" (1.5 cm)

Back (rs)

Backstitch

Front (rs)

(ws)

6 Make the button loops and attach to the front, then attach the buttons to the back

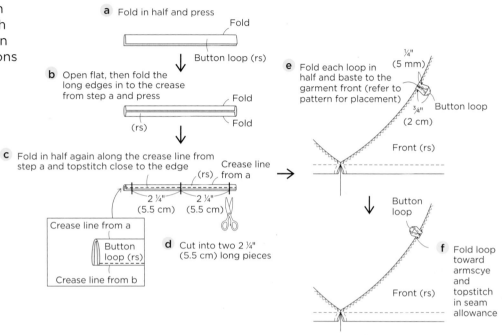

a Fold in half and press

Fold

Button loop (rs)

b Open flat, then fold the long edges in to the crease from step a and press

Fold

(rs)

Fold

c Fold in half again along the crease line from step a and topstitch close to the edge

Crease line from a

(rs)

2 ¼" (5.5 cm)   2 ¼" (5.5 cm)

Crease line from a

Button loop (rs)

Crease line from b

d Cut into two 2 ¼" (5.5 cm) long pieces

e Fold each loop in half and baste to the garment front (refer to pattern for placement)

¼" (5 mm)

Button loop

¾" (2 cm)

Front (rs)

Button loop

f Fold loop toward armscye and topstitch in seam allowance

Front (rs)

7 Make the drawstring and insert through casing

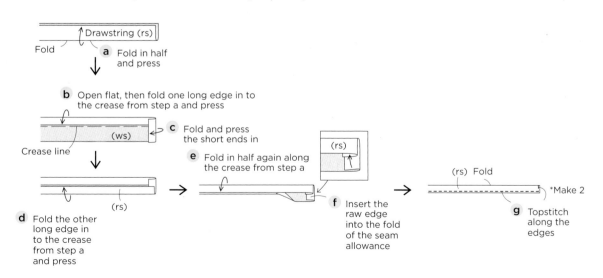

Drawstring (rs)

Fold

a Fold in half and press

b Open flat, then fold one long edge in to the crease from step a and press

(ws)

Crease line

(rs)

c Fold and press the short ends in

e Fold in half again along the crease from step a

(rs)

f Insert the raw edge into the fold of the seam allowance

d Fold the other long edge in to the crease from step a and press

(rs) Fold

*Make 2

g Topstitch along the edges

J | Wide Leg Pants

Shown on pages 10, 15, 17 and 43

K | Farmer's Pants

Shown on pages 27 and 37

Finished Sizes

	S	M	L	XL
Waist for J and K	25 ¼"-33 ¼" (64-84.5cm)	26 ½"-34 ½" (67.4-87.9 cm)	27 ¾"-35 ¾" (70.4-90.9 cm)	29 ¼"-37 ¼" (74.4-94.9 cm)
Length J	37 ¼" (94.5 cm)	37 ¾" (96 cm)	38 ½" (97.5 cm)	39" (99 cm)
Length K	35 ¼" (89.5 cm)	35 ¾" (91 cm)	36 ½" (92.5 cm)	37" (94 cm)

Materials

For J

- 41" (106 cm) wide linen or cotton silk (see chart at right for yardage)
- Fusible interfacing (see chart at right for dimensions)
- 2" (5 cm) wide elastic tape (see chart at right for length)

	S	M	L	XL
Fabric Requirements	2 ¾ yds (2.4 m)	2 ¾ yds (2.4 m)	2 ¾ yds (2.4 m)	3 yds (2.6 m)
Fusible Interfacing Requirements	6" x 15 ¾" (6 x 40 cm)	6" x 15 ¾" (6 x 40 cm)	6" x 15 ¾" (6 x 40 cm)	6" x 17 ¾" (6 x 45 cm)
Elastic Tape Requirements	13 ¾" (35 cm)	14 ¼" (36 cm)	14 ½" (37 cm)	15" (36 cm)

For K

- 41" (106 cm) wide linen (see chart at right for yardage)
- Fusible interfacing (see chart at right for dimensions)
- 2" (5 cm) wide elastic tape (see chart at right for length)

	S	M	L	XL
Fabric Requirements	2 ½ yds (2.3 m)	2 ½ yds (2.3 m)	2 ½ yds (2.3 m)	2 ¾ yds (2.5 m)
Fusible Interfacing Requirements	6" x 15 ¾" (6 x 40 cm)	6" x 15 ¾" (6 x 40 cm)	6" x 15 ¾" (6 x 40 cm)	6" x 17 ¾" (6 x 45 cm)
Elastic Tape Requirements	13 ¾" (35 cm)	14 ¼" (36 cm)	14 ½" (37 cm)	15" (36 cm)

Pattern Pieces on Sheet 6

☐ Front   ☐ Back   ☐ Pocket   ☐ Front waistband   ☐ Back waistband

Pattern Layout

For J

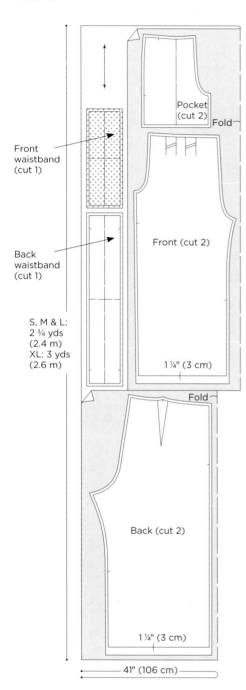

Front waistband (cut 1)

Back waistband (cut 1)

Pocket (cut 2)

Fold

Front (cut 2)

1 ¼" (3 cm)

Fold

Back (cut 2)

1 ¼" (3 cm)

S, M & L:
2 ¾ yds
(2.4 m)
XL: 3 yds
(2.6 m)

41" (106 cm)

For K

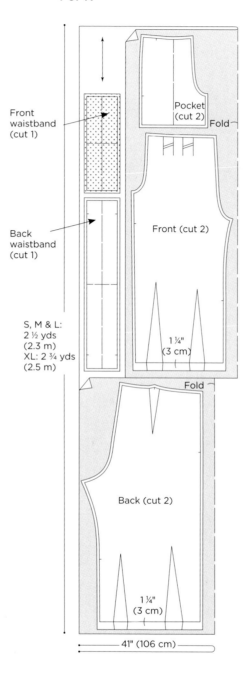

Front waistband (cut 1)

Back waistband (cut 1)

Pocket (cut 2)

Fold

Front (cut 2)

1 ¼" (3 cm)

Fold

Back (cut 2)

1 ¼" (3 cm)

S, M & L:
2 ½ yds
(2.3 m)
XL: 2 ¾ yds
(2.5 m)

41" (106 cm)

- Add ⅜" (1 cm) seam allowance, unless otherwise noted.
- Cut out and adhere fusible interfacing to the wrong side of the fabric for the areas shaded with ▒.

Construction Steps

1. Sew the pleats and darts along the waistline. For K, sew the pleats along the hemline as well (see page 85).

2. Make the pockets (see page 86).

3. Sew the side seams (see page 87).

4. Sew the inseams (see page 87).

5. Sew the rise (see page 88).

6. Make the waistband (see page 88).

7. Attach the waistband (see page 89).

8. Hem the pants (see page 89).

Sew using ⅜" (1 cm) seam allowance, unless otherwise noted.

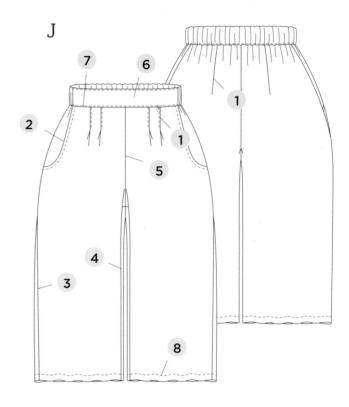

J

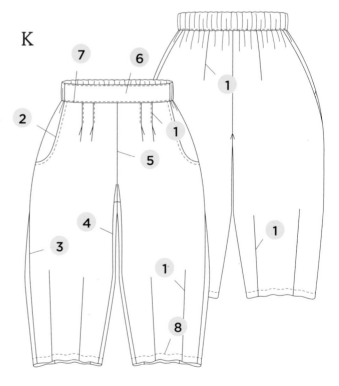

K

1 Sew the pleats and darts along the waistline. For K, sew the pleats along the hemline as well

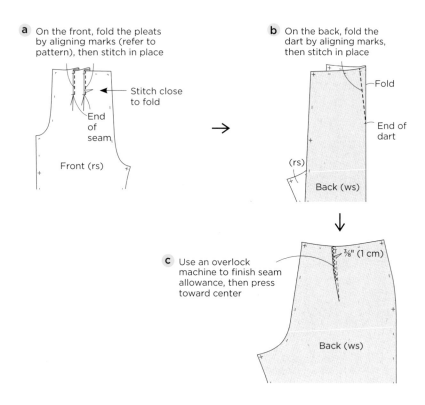

a On the front, fold the pleats by aligning marks (refer to pattern), then stitch in place

Stitch close to fold

End of seam

Front (rs)

b On the back, fold the dart by aligning marks, then stitch in place

Fold

End of dart

(rs)

Back (ws)

c Use an overlock machine to finish seam allowance, then press toward center

⅜" (1 cm)

Back (ws)

For K Only

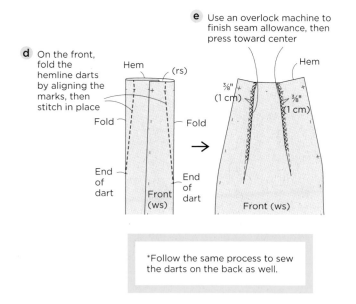

d On the front, fold the hemline darts by aligning the marks, then stitch in place

Hem

(rs)

Fold

Fold

End of dart

End of dart

Front (ws)

e Use an overlock machine to finish seam allowance, then press toward center

Hem

⅜" (1 cm)

⅜" (1 cm)

Front (ws)

*Follow the same process to sew the darts on the back as well.

2 Make the pockets

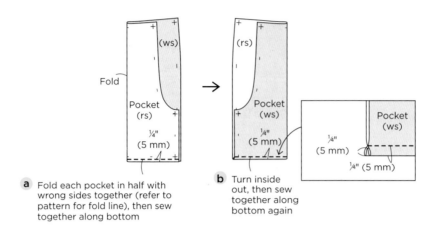

a Fold each pocket in half with wrong sides together (refer to pattern for fold line), then sew together along bottom

b Turn inside out, then sew together along bottom again

c Turn each pocket right side out, align on top of pants front, and sew bottom layer of pocket in place

e Turn each pocket inside out and fold to wrong side of pants front, pressing so seam is visible on wrong side of pants

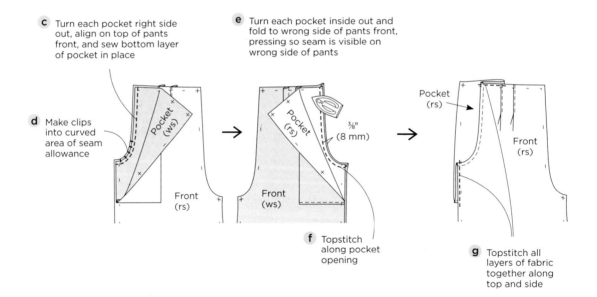

d Make clips into curved area of seam allowance

f Topstitch along pocket opening

g Topstitch all layers of fabric together along top and side

3 Sew the side seams

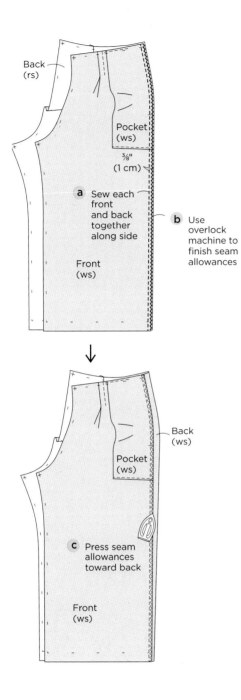

Back (rs)

Pocket (ws)

⅜" (1 cm)

a Sew each front and back together along side

b Use overlock machine to finish seam allowances

Front (ws)

Back (ws)

Pocket (ws)

c Press seam allowances toward back

Front (ws)

4 Sew the inseams

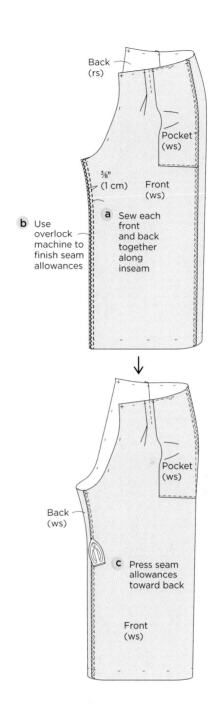

Back (rs)

Pocket (ws)

⅜" (1 cm)

Front (ws)

b Use overlock machine to finish seam allowances

a Sew each front and back together along inseam

Back (ws)

Pocket (ws)

c Press seam allowances toward back

Front (ws)

5 Sew the rise

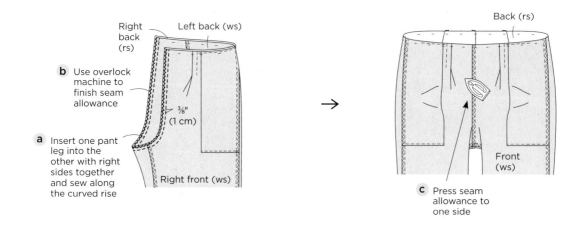

Right back (rs)

Left back (ws)

Back (rs)

b Use overlock machine to finish seam allowance

a Insert one pant leg into the other with right sides together and sew along the curved rise

⅜" (1 cm)

Right front (ws)

Front (ws)

c Press seam allowance to one side

6 Make the waistband

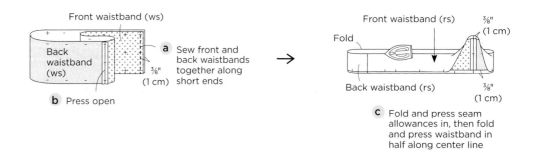

Front waistband (ws)

Back waistband (ws)

a Sew front and back waistbands together along short ends

b Press open

⅜" (1 cm)

Front waistband (rs)

⅜" (1 cm)

Fold

Back waistband (rs)

⅜" (1 cm)

c Fold and press seam allowances in, then fold and press waistband in half along center line

7 Attach the waistband

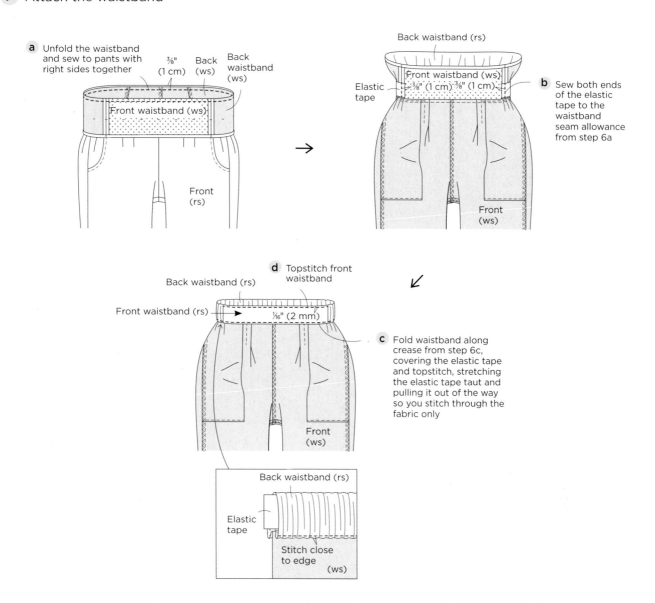

a Unfold the waistband and sew to pants with right sides together

³⁄₈" (1 cm)

Back (ws)

Back waistband (ws)

Front waistband (ws)

Front (rs)

→

Back waistband (rs)

Front waistband (ws)

Elastic tape

³⁄₈" (1 cm) ³⁄₈" (1 cm)

b Sew both ends of the elastic tape to the waistband seam allowance from step 6a

Front (ws)

↙

d Topstitch front waistband

Back waistband (rs)

Front waistband (rs) → ¹⁄₁₆" (2 mm)

c Fold waistband along crease from step 6c, covering the elastic tape and topstitch, stretching the elastic tape taut and pulling it out of the way so you stitch through the fabric only

Front (ws)

Back waistband (rs)

Elastic tape

Stitch close to edge

(ws)

8 Hem the pants

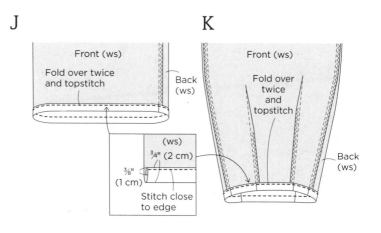

J

Front (ws)

Fold over twice and topstitch

Back (ws)

(ws)

³⁄₄" (2 cm)

³⁄₈" (1 cm)

Stitch close to edge

K

Front (ws)

Fold over twice and topstitch

Back (ws)

L | Wrap Front Pants

Shown on pages 13, 25, 28 and 40

Finished Sizes

	S	M	L	XL
Waist	24 ¾"-32 ¾" (63-83.5 cm)	26 ¾"-34 ¾" (68-88.5 cm)	28 ¼"-36 ¼" (72-92.5 cm)	30 ¾"-38 ¾" (78-98.5 cm)
Length	35 ¾" (91 cm)	36 ½" (92.5 cm)	37" (94 cm)	37 ¾" (95.5 cm)

Materials

- 41" (104 cm) wide linen (see chart below for yardage)
- 6" x 9 ¾" (15 x 25 cm) of fusible interfacing
- 1 ½" (4 cm) wide elastic tape (see chart below for length)

	S	M	L	XL
Fabric Requirements	2 ½ yds (2.3 m)	2 ½ yds (2.3 m)	2 ½ yds (2.3 m)	2 ¾ yds (2.4 m)
Elastic Tape Requirements	18 ½" (47 cm)	20" (51 cm)	21 ¼" (54 cm)	23 ¼" (59 cm)

Pattern Pieces on Sheet 3

- ☐ Right front
- ☐ Left front
- ☐ Back
- ☐ Pocket
- ☐ Front waistband
- ☐ Back waistband

Sew using ⅜" (1 cm) seam allowance, unless otherwise noted.

Construction Steps

1. Make the pockets (see page 91).

2. Sew the side seams and inseams (see page 91).

3. Sew the rise (see step 5 on page 88).

4. Fold the pleat on the right front (see page 91).

5. Make and attach the waistband (see steps 6 and 7 on pages 88 and 89).

6. Hem the pants (see step 8 on page 89).

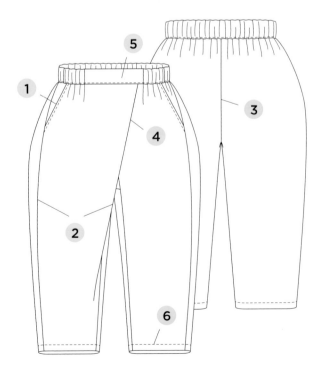

Pattern Layout

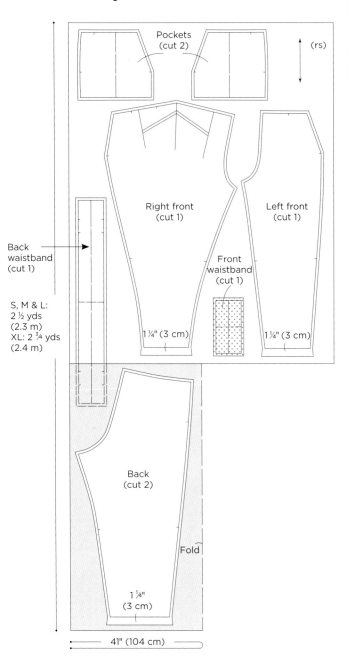

Pockets (cut 2)

(rs)

Right front (cut 1)

Left front (cut 1)

Back waistband (cut 1)

Front waistband (cut 1)

S, M & L: 2 ½ yds (2.3 m)
XL: 2 ¾ yds (2.4 m)

1 ¼" (3 cm)   1 ¼" (3 cm)

Back (cut 2)

Fold

1 ¼" (3 cm)

41" (104 cm)

- Add ⅜" (1 cm) seam allowance, unless otherwise noted.
- Cut out and adhere fusible interfacing to the wrong side of the fabric for the areas shaded with ⬚.

1 Make the pockets

Refer to step 2 on page 86 for instructions on making the pocket, but use ¼" (5 mm) seam allowance when topstitching

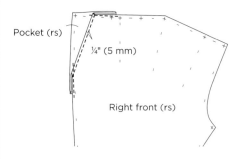

Pocket (rs)

¼" (5 mm)

Right front (rs)

2 Sew the side seams and inseams

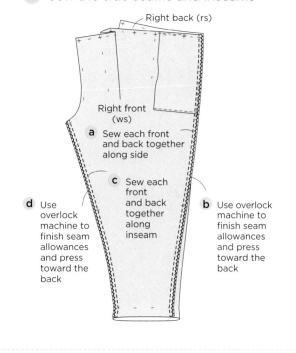

Right back (rs)

Right front (ws)

a Sew each front and back together along side

c Sew each front and back together along inseam

d Use overlock machine to finish seam allowances and press toward the back

b Use overlock machine to finish seam allowances and press toward the back

4 Fold the pleat on the right front

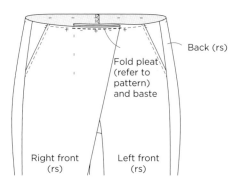

Back (rs)

Fold pleat (refer to pattern) and baste

Right front (rs)

Left front (rs)

M │ Antique Skirt

Shown on pages 29, 30 and 45

Finished Sizes

	S	M	L	XL
Waist	23 ¾"-31 ¾" (60.4-80.9 cm)	25 ¾"-33 ¾" (65.5-86 cm)	27 ½"-35 ½" (70-90.5 cm)	30"-38" (76-96.5 cm)
Length	31 ¾" (80.5 cm)	32 ¼" (82 cm)	33" (83.5 cm)	33 ½" (85 cm)

Materials

- 41" (104 cm) wide lyocell or linen (see chart below for yardage)
- 19 ¾" x 8" (50 x 20 cm) of fusible interfacing
- 1 ½" (4 cm) wide elastic tape (see chart below for length)

	S	M	L	XL
Fabric Requirements	2 ½ yds (2.2 m)	2 ½ yds (2.2 m)	2 ½ yds (2.2 m)	2 ½ yds (2.3 m)
Elastic Tape Requirements	12 ¼" (31 cm)	13 ½" (34 cm)	14 ¼" (36 cm)	15 ½" (39 cm)

Pattern Pieces on Sheet 4

- ☐ Front
- ☐ Back
- ☐ Front waistband
- ☐ Back waistband
- ☐ Pocket
- ☐ Pocket placket

- Add ⅜" (1 cm) seam allowance, unless otherwise noted.
- Do not add seam allowance to areas marked 0.
- Cut out and adhere fusible interfacing to the wrong side of the fabric for the areas shaded with ▦.

Pattern Layout

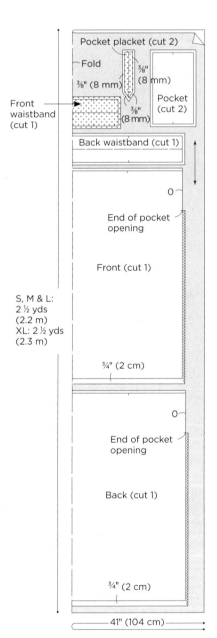

Construction Steps

1   Sew the side seams (see diagram below).

2   Make the pockets (see page 94).

3   Make gathers along the waistline (see page 94).

4   Make the waistband (see page 94).

5   Attach the waistband (see page 95).

6   Hem the skirt (see page 95).

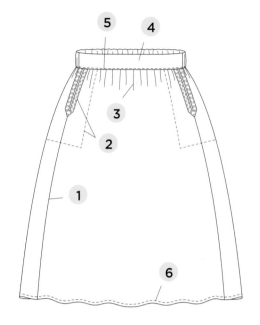

Sew using ⅜" (1 cm) seam allowance, unless otherwise noted.

1   Sew the side seams

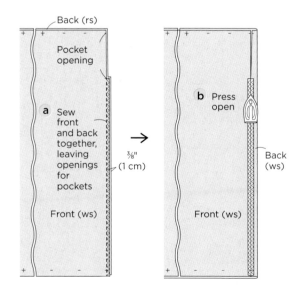

Back (rs)

Pocket opening

a   Sew front and back together, leaving openings for pockets

⅜" (1 cm)

Front (ws)

b   Press open

Back (ws)

Front (ws)

2 Make the pockets

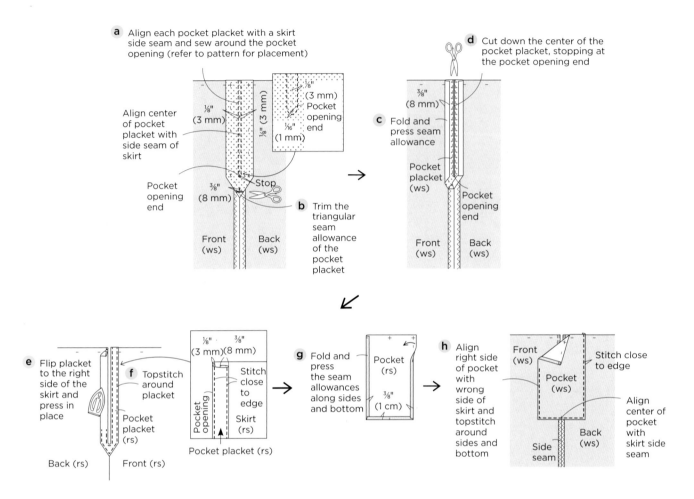

a Align each pocket placket with a skirt side seam and sew around the pocket opening (refer to pattern for placement)

Align center of pocket placket with side seam of skirt

Pocket opening end

⅛" (3 mm)

⅛" (3 mm)

⅛" (3 mm)

1/16" (1 mm)

Pocket opening end

⅜" (8 mm)

Stop

Front (ws)

Back (ws)

b Trim the triangular seam allowance of the pocket placket

d Cut down the center of the pocket placket, stopping at the pocket opening end

⅜" (8 mm)

c Fold and press seam allowance

Pocket placket (ws)

Pocket opening end

Front (ws)

Back (ws)

e Flip placket to the right side of the skirt and press in place

Back (rs)

Front (rs)

Pocket placket (rs)

f Topstitch around placket

⅛" (3 mm)

⅜" (8 mm)

Stitch close to edge

Pocket opening

Skirt (rs)

Pocket placket (rs)

g Fold and press the seam allowances along sides and bottom

Pocket (rs)

⅜" (1 cm)

h Align right side of pocket with wrong side of skirt and topstitch around sides and bottom

Front (ws)

Pocket (ws)

Stitch close to edge

Align center of pocket with skirt side seam

Side seam

Back (ws)

3 Make gathers along the waistline

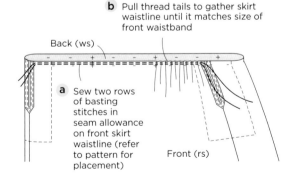

b Pull thread tails to gather skirt waistline until it matches size of front waistband

Back (ws)

a Sew two rows of basting stitches in seam allowance on front skirt waistline (refer to pattern for placement)

Front (rs)

4 Make the waistband

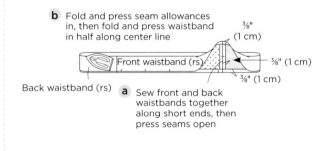

b Fold and press seam allowances in, then fold and press waistband in half along center line

Front waistband (rs)

⅜" (1 cm)

⅜" (1 cm)

⅜" (1 cm)

Back waistband (rs)

a Sew front and back waistbands together along short ends, then press seams open

5 Attach the waistband

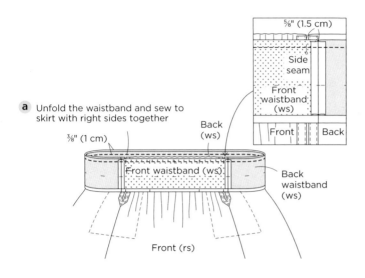

a Unfold the waistband and sew to skirt with right sides together

⅝" (1.5 cm)

Side seam

Front waistband (ws)

Front | Back

Back (ws)

⅜" (1 cm)

Front waistband (ws)

Back waistband (ws)

Front (rs)

b Sew both ends of elastic tape to the waistband seam allowance from step 4a

c Fold waistband along crease from step 4b, covering the elastic tape and topstitch, stretching the elastic tape taut and pulling it out of the way so you stitch through the fabric only

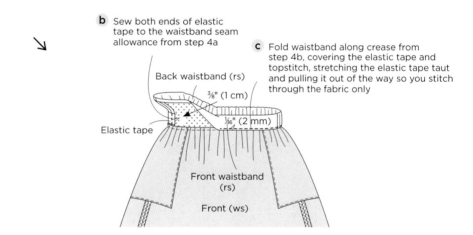

Back waistband (rs)

⅜" (1 cm)

Elastic tape

1/16" (2 mm)

Front waistband (rs)

Front (ws)

6 Hem the skirt

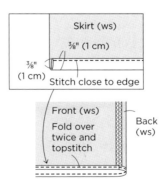

Skirt (ws)

⅜" (1 cm)

⅜" (1 cm)

Stitch close to edge

Front (ws)

Fold over twice and topstitch

Back (ws)

I | V-Neck Tunic

Shown on pages 38, 39 and 41

Finished Sizes

	S	M	L	XL
Bust	50 ¾" (128.8 cm)	52 ¾" (134 cm)	54 ¼" (138 cm)	56 ¾" (144 cm)
Sleeve Length	10 ¼" (26 cm)	10 ½" (26.5 cm)	10 ¾" (27 cm)	10 ¾" (27.5 cm)
Length	38 ½" (98 cm)	39 ¼" (99.5 cm)	39 ¾" (101 cm)	40 ½" (103 cm)

Materials

• 41" (104 cm) wide linen or cotton silk (see chart below for yardage)

	S	M	L	XL
Fabric Requirements	3 ¼ yds (2.9 m)	3 ¼ yds (2.9 m)	3 ¼ yds (2.9 m)	3 ½ yds (3 m)

Pattern Pieces on Sheet 6

☐ Front*

☐ Back*

☐ Sleeve

*Note that both the front and back are divided into two pieces in order to fit on the pattern sheet, and will need to be taped together for the complete pattern.

There is no pattern piece for the neckline bias strip. Cut following the dimensions listed below:

	S	M	L	XL
Neckline bias strip (cut 1 on the bias)	¾" x 28 ¼" (2 x 71.5 cm)	¾" x 28 ½" (2 x 72.5 cm)	¾" x 29 ¼" (2 x 74 cm)	¾" x 30" (2 x 76 cm)

Pattern Layout

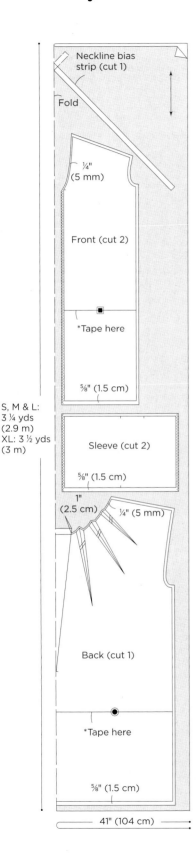

Neckline bias strip (cut 1)

Fold

¼" (5 mm)

Front (cut 2)

*Tape here

⅝" (1.5 cm)

S, M & L: 3 ¼ yds (2.9 m)
XL: 3 ½ yds (3 m)

Sleeve (cut 2)

⅝" (1.5 cm)

1" (2.5 cm)

¼" (5 mm)

Back (cut 1)

*Tape here

⅝" (1.5 cm)

41" (104 cm)

Construction Steps

1. Sew the darts on the back (see page 98).

2. Sew the shoulders (see page 99).

3. Finish the neckline with the bias strip (see page 99).

4. Sew the center front seam (see page 100).

5. Sew the side seams (see page 100).

6. Make the sleeves (see page 101).

7. Hem the dress (see page 101).

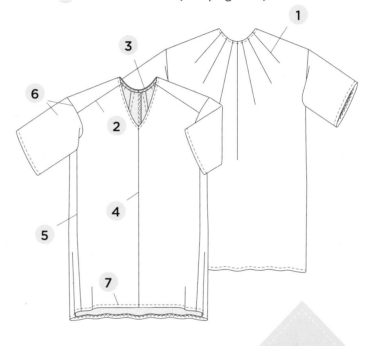

Sew using ⅜" (1 cm) seam allowance, unless otherwise noted.

- Add ⅜" (1 cm) seam allowance, unless otherwise noted.
- Use an overlock machine to finish the raw edges of the front and sleeve, as shown in the above diagram.

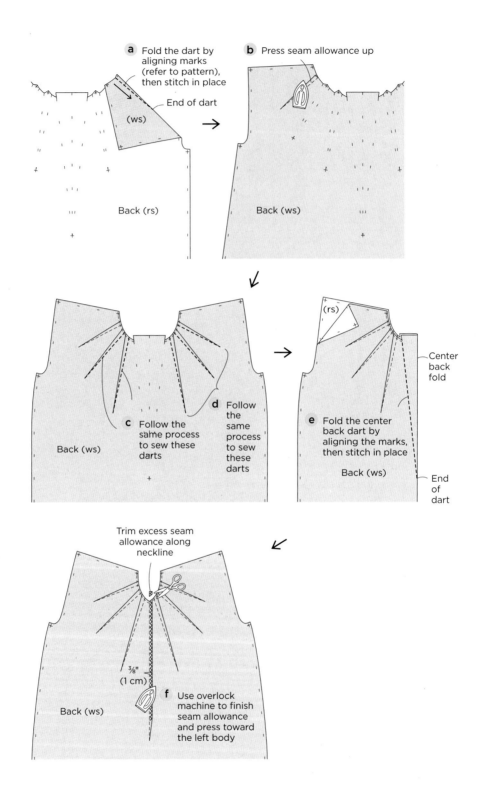

a Fold the dart by aligning marks (refer to pattern), then stitch in place

End of dart

(ws)

Back (rs)

b Press seam allowance up

Back (ws)

c Follow the same process to sew these darts

Back (ws)

d Follow the same process to sew these darts

e Fold the center back dart by aligning the marks, then stitch in place

(rs)

Center back fold

End of dart

Back (ws)

Trim excess seam allowance along neckline

⅜" (1 cm)

f Use overlock machine to finish seam allowance and press toward the left body

Back (ws)

2 Sew the shoulders

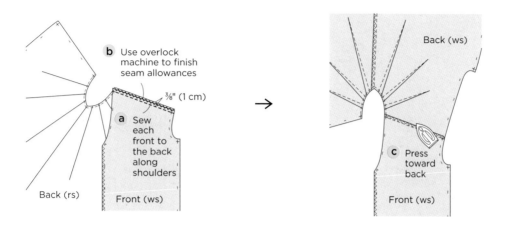

b Use overlock machine to finish seam allowances

⅜" (1 cm)

a Sew each front to the back along shoulders

Back (rs)

Front (ws)

Back (ws)

c Press toward back

Front (ws)

3 Finish the neckline with the bias strip

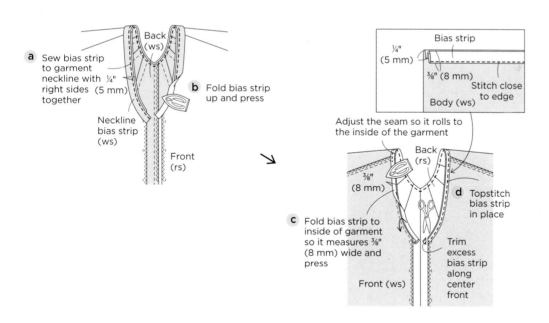

a Sew bias strip to garment neckline with ¼" (5 mm) right sides together

Back (ws)

b Fold bias strip up and press

Neckline bias strip (ws)

Front (rs)

Bias strip

¼" (5 mm)

⅜" (8 mm)

Stitch close to edge

Body (ws)

Adjust the seam so it rolls to the inside of the garment

Back (rs)

⅜" (8 mm)

d Topstitch bias strip in place

c Fold bias strip to inside of garment so it measures ⅜" (8 mm) wide and press

Trim excess bias strip along center front

Front (ws)

4 Sew the center front seam

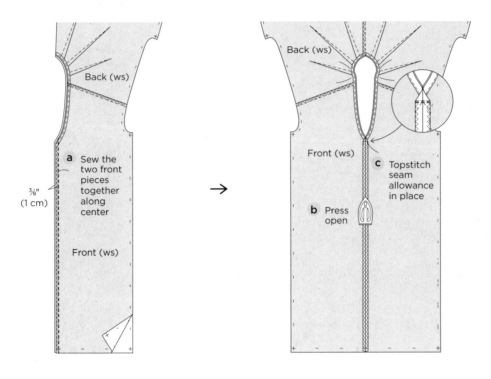

Back (ws)

a Sew the two front pieces together along center

⅜"
(1 cm)

Front (ws)

Back (ws)

Front (ws)

b Press open

c Topstitch seam allowance in place

---

5 Sew the side seams

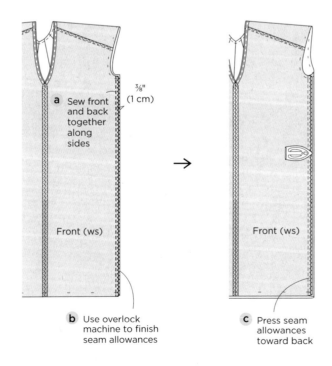

a Sew front and back together along sides

⅜"
(1 cm)

Front (ws)

b Use overlock machine to finish seam allowances

Front (ws)

c Press seam allowances toward back

6 Make the sleeves

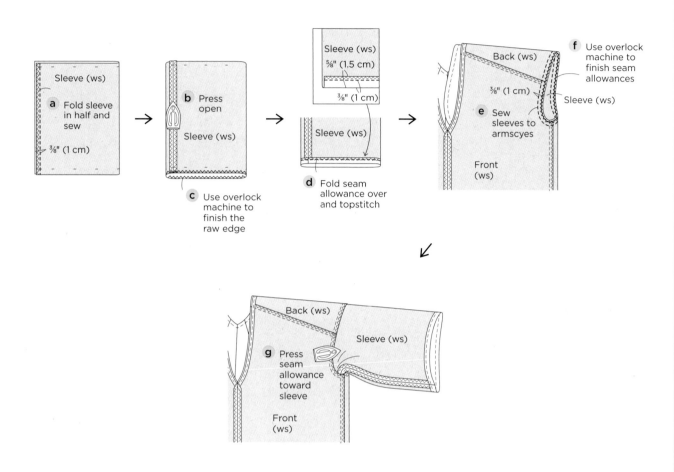

a Fold sleeve in half and sew

Sleeve (ws)

⅜" (1 cm)

b Press open

Sleeve (ws)

c Use overlock machine to finish the raw edge

Sleeve (ws)

⅝" (1.5 cm)

⅜" (1 cm)

Sleeve (ws)

d Fold seam allowance over and topstitch

Back (ws)

f Use overlock machine to finish seam allowances

⅜" (1 cm)

Sleeve (ws)

e Sew sleeves to armscyes

Front (ws)

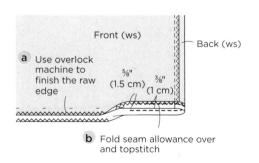

Back (ws)

Sleeve (ws)

g Press seam allowance toward sleeve

Front (ws)

7 Hem the dress

Front (ws)

Back (ws)

a Use overlock machine to finish the raw edge

⅝" (1.5 cm)

⅜" (1 cm)

b Fold seam allowance over and topstitch

F | Stand Collar Dress

Shown on pages 20, 21 and 34

Finished Sizes

	S	M	L	XL
Bust	53" (135 cm)	55" (139.8 cm)	56 ¾" (143.8 cm)	59" (149.8 cm)
Length	39 ¾" (101 cm)	40 ½" (102.5 cm)	41 ¼"(104.5 cm)	42" (106.5 cm)

Materials

- 41" (104 cm) wide cotton double gauze, linen, or cotton/linen blend (see chart below for yardage)
- 23 ¾" x 4" (60 x 10 cm) of fusible interfacing
- Two ⅜" (1 cm) diameter buttons

	S	M	L	XL
Fabric Requirements	3 ¼ yds (2.9 m)	3 ¼ yds (2.9 m)	3 ¼ yds (2.9 m)	3 ½ yds (3 m)

Pattern Pieces on Sheet 1

- ☐ Front*
- ☐ Back*
- ☐ Pocket
- ☐ Collar

*Note that both the front and back are divided into two pieces in order to fit on the pattern sheet, and will need to be taped together for the complete pattern.

There is no pattern piece for the button loop. Cut following the dimensions listed below:

- ☐ Button loop (cut 1 on the bias): 5 ¼" x ¾" (13 x 1.8 cm)

- Add ⅜" (1 cm) seam allowance, unless otherwise noted.
- Use an overlock machine to finish the raw edges of the front, back, and pockets, as shown in the above diagram.
- Cut out and adhere fusible interfacing to the wrong side of the fabric for the areas shaded with ⬚⬚⬚.

Pattern Layout

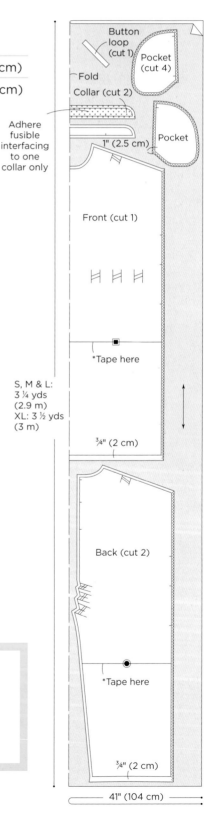

Button loop (cut 1)

Pocket (cut 4)

Fold

Collar (cut 2)

Adhere fusible interfacing to one collar only

1" (2.5 cm)

Pocket

Front (cut 1)

*Tape here

S, M & L: 3 ¼ yds (2.9 m)
XL: 3 ½ yds (3 m)

¾" (2 cm)

Back (cut 2)

*Tape here

¾" (2 cm)

41" (104 cm)

Construction Steps

1. Sew the waist tucks on the front (see diagram below).

2. Sew the waist tucks on the back pieces, and then sew the back pieces together (see page 104).

3. Make the button loops (see page 105).

4. Sew the shoulder tucks, and then sew the front and back together at the shoulders (see page 105).

5. Make the collar (see page 106).

6. Make the pockets and sew the side seams (see page 107).

7. Finish the sleeve openings (see page 108).

8. Hem the dress (see page 108).

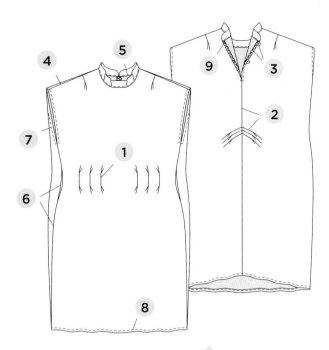

Sew using ⅜" (1 cm) seam allowance, unless otherwise noted.

---

1 Sew the waist tucks on the front

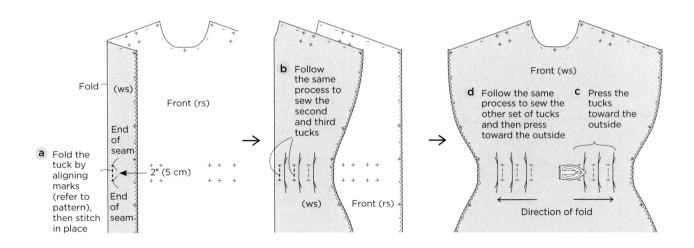

a Fold the tuck by aligning marks (refer to pattern), then stitch in place

Fold

(ws)

Front (rs)

End of seam

2" (5 cm)

End of seam

b Follow the same process to sew the second and third tucks

(ws)   Front (rs)

c Press the tucks toward the outside

d Follow the same process to sew the other set of tucks and then press toward the outside

Front (ws)

Direction of fold

2 Sew the waist tucks on the back pieces, and then sew the back pieces together

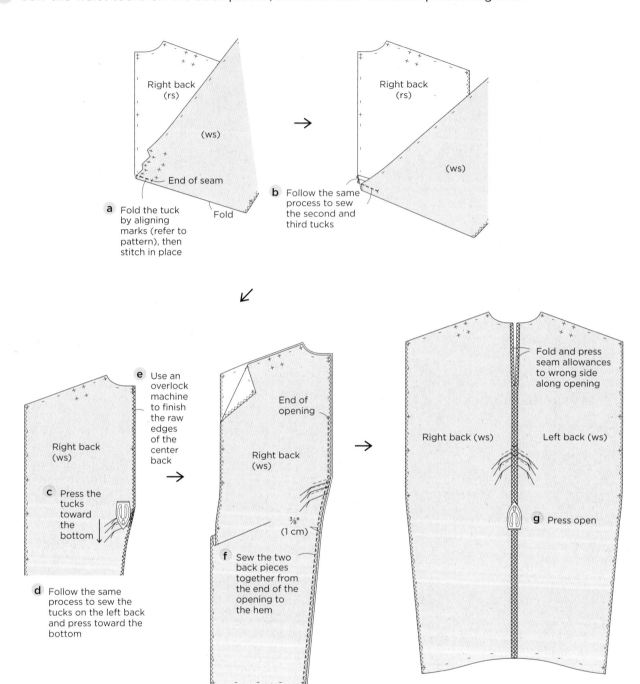

Right back (rs)

(ws)

End of seam

a Fold the tuck by aligning marks (refer to pattern), then stitch in place

Fold

Right back (rs)

(ws)

b Follow the same process to sew the second and third tucks

Right back (ws)

e Use an overlock machine to finish the raw edges of the center back

c Press the tucks toward the bottom

d Follow the same process to sew the tucks on the left back and press toward the bottom

End of opening

Right back (ws)

3/8" (1 cm)

f Sew the two back pieces together from the end of the opening to the hem

Fold and press seam allowances to wrong side along opening

Right back (ws)

Left back (ws)

g Press open

3 Make the button loops

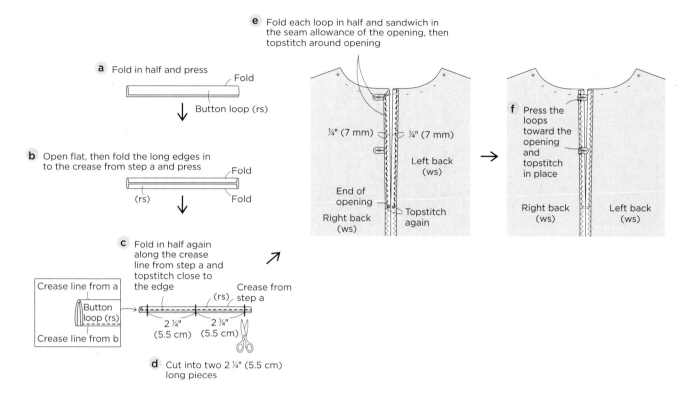

a Fold in half and press

Fold

Button loop (rs)

b Open flat, then fold the long edges in to the crease from step a and press

Fold

(rs)

Fold

c Fold in half again along the crease line from step a and topstitch close to the edge

Crease line from a

Button loop (rs)

Crease line from b

(rs)

Crease from step a

2 ¼" (5.5 cm)   2 ¼" (5.5 cm)

d Cut into two 2 ¼" (5.5 cm) long pieces

e Fold each loop in half and sandwich in the seam allowance of the opening, then topstitch around opening

¼" (7 mm)   ¼" (7 mm)

Left back (ws)

End of opening

Right back (ws)

Topstitch again

f Press the loops toward the opening and topstitch in place

Right back (ws)

Left back (ws)

4 Sew the shoulder tucks, and then sew the front and back together at the shoulders

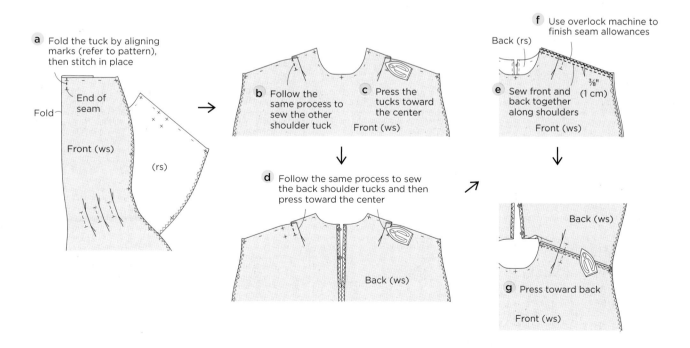

a Fold the tuck by aligning marks (refer to pattern), then stitch in place

End of seam

Fold

Front (ws)

(rs)

b Follow the same process to sew the other shoulder tuck

c Press the tucks toward the center

Front (ws)

d Follow the same process to sew the back shoulder tucks and then press toward the center

Back (ws)

f Use overlock machine to finish seam allowances

Back (rs)

e Sew front and back together along shoulders

Front (ws)

⅜" (1 cm)

Back (ws)

g Press toward back

Front (ws)

5 Make the collar

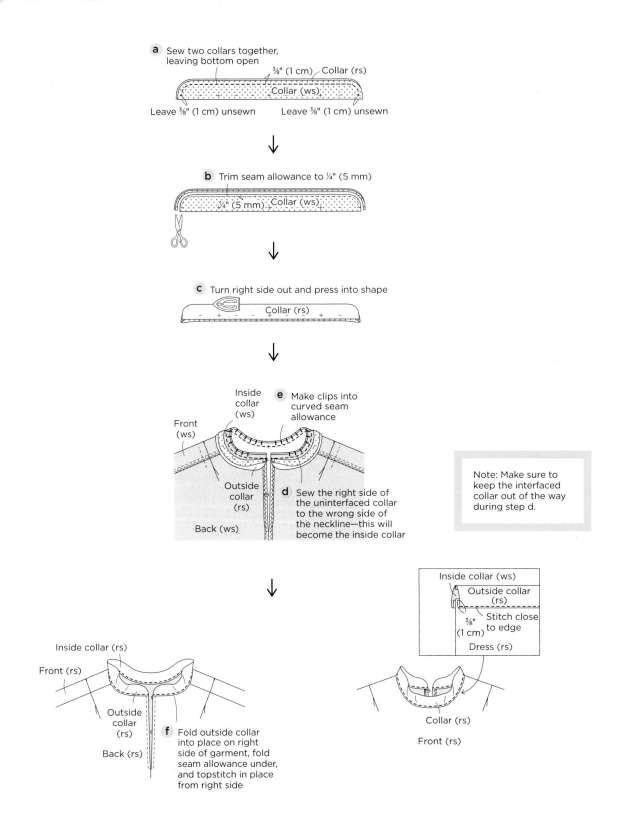

a Sew two collars together, leaving bottom open

⅜" (1 cm)   Collar (rs)

Collar (ws)

Leave ⅜" (1 cm) unsewn   Leave ⅜" (1 cm) unsewn

b Trim seam allowance to ¼" (5 mm)

¼" (5 mm)   Collar (ws)

c Turn right side out and press into shape

Collar (rs)

Inside collar (ws)

e Make clips into curved seam allowance

Front (ws)

Outside collar (rs)

Back (ws)

d Sew the right side of the uninterfaced collar to the wrong side of the neckline—this will become the inside collar

Note: Make sure to keep the interfaced collar out of the way during step d.

Inside collar (rs)

Front (rs)

Outside collar (rs)

Back (rs)

f Fold outside collar into place on right side of garment, fold seam allowance under, and topstitch in place from right side

Inside collar (ws)

Outside collar (rs)

⅜" (1 cm)   Stitch close to edge

Dress (rs)

Collar (rs)

Front (rs)

6 Make the pockets and sew the side seams

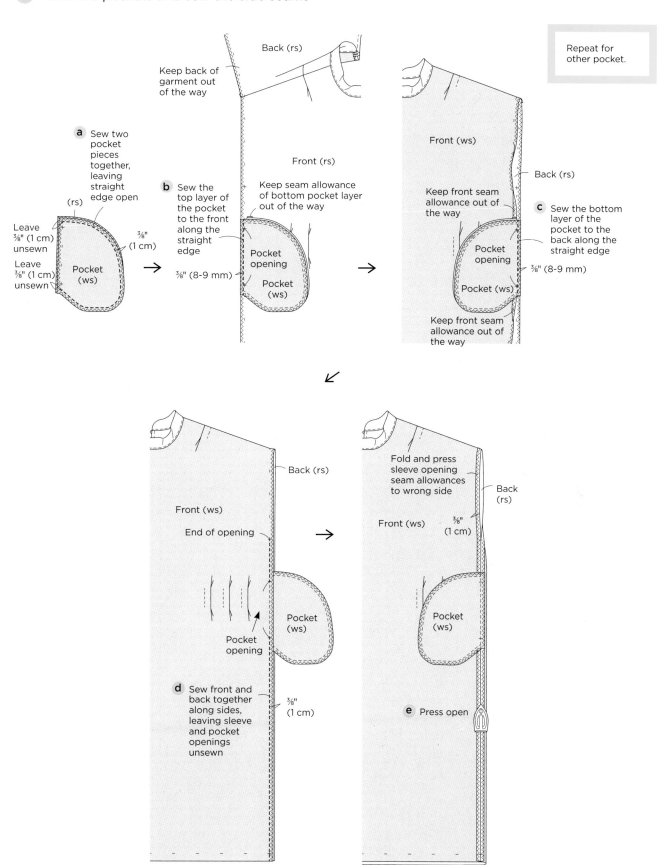

Repeat for other pocket.

a Sew two pocket pieces together, leaving straight edge open

(rs)

Leave ³⁄₈" (1 cm) unsewn

Leave ³⁄₈" (1 cm) unsewn

Pocket (ws)

³⁄₈" (1 cm)

Back (rs)

Keep back of garment out of the way

Front (rs)

b Sew the top layer of the pocket to the front along the straight edge

³⁄₈" (8-9 mm)

Keep seam allowance of bottom pocket layer out of the way

Pocket opening

Pocket (ws)

Front (ws)

Keep front seam allowance out of the way

Back (rs)

c Sew the bottom layer of the pocket to the back along the straight edge

³⁄₈" (8-9 mm)

Pocket opening

Pocket (ws)

Keep front seam allowance out of the way

Back (rs)

Front (ws)

End of opening

Pocket opening

Pocket (ws)

d Sew front and back together along sides, leaving sleeve and pocket openings unsewn

³⁄₈" (1 cm)

Fold and press sleeve opening seam allowances to wrong side

Front (ws)

³⁄₈" (1 cm)

Back (rs)

Pocket (ws)

e Press open

7 Finish the sleeve openings

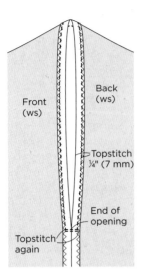

Front (ws)

Back (ws)

Topstitch ¼" (7 mm)

End of opening

Topstitch again

8 Hem the dress

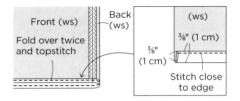

Front (ws)

Fold over twice and topstitch

Back (ws)

(ws)

⅜" (1 cm)

⅜" (1 cm)

Stitch close to edge

G | Two Way Tunic Shirt   H | Two Way Tunic Dress

Shown on pages 14, 37 and 40   *Shown on page 27*

Finished Sizes

For G

	S	M	L	XL
Bust	52 ½" (133 cm)	54 ¼" (138 cm)	56" (142 cm)	58 ¼" (148 cm)
Sleeve Length	2 ½" (6.2 cm)	2 ½" (6.4 cm)	2 ½" (6.5 cm)	2 ¾" (6.7 cm)
Length	22 ¼" (56.5 cm)	22 ¾" (57.5 cm)	23" (58.5 cm)	23 ¾" (60 cm)

For H

	S	M	L	XL
Bust	52 ¾" (134 cm)	54 ¾" (138.8 cm)	55" (139.8 cm)	57" (145 cm)
Sleeve Length	2 ½" (6.2 cm)	2 ½" (6.4 cm)	2 ½" (6.5 cm)	2 ¾" (6.7 cm)
Length	38 ¼" (97 cm)	38 ¾" (98.5 cm)	39 ½" (100.5 cm)	40 ½" (102.5 cm)

Materials

For Both

- 41" (106 cm) wide cotton double gauze, linen, cotton silk, or lyocell (see chart below for yardage)
- 25 ½" x 8" (65 x 20 cm) of fusible interfacing
- Two ½" (1.3 cm) diameter buttons

For G

	S	M	L	XL
Fabric Requirements	2 yds (1.7 m)	2 yds (1.7 m)	2 yds (1.7 m)	2 yds (1.8 m)

For H

	S	M	L	XL
Fabric Requirements	2 ¾ yds (2.5 m)	3 yds (2.6 m)	3 yds (2.6 m)	3 yds (2.6 m)

Pattern Pieces on Sheet 2

- ☐ Front*
- ☐ Back*
- ☐ Top and bottom placket
- ☐ Sleeve
- ☐ Collar

*Note that for H, both the front and back are divided into two pieces in order to fit on the pattern sheet, and will need to be taped together for the complete pattern.

Pattern Layout

For G

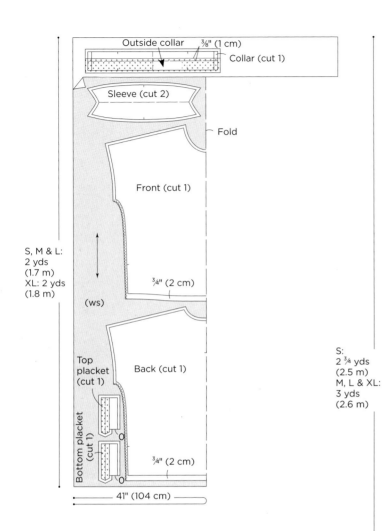

For G diagram labels:
- Outside collar — ⅜" (1 cm)
- Collar (cut 1)
- Sleeve (cut 2)
- Fold
- Front (cut 1)
- ¾" (2 cm)
- (ws)
- Back (cut 1)
- Top placket (cut 1)
- Bottom placket (cut 1)
- ¾" (2 cm)
- S, M & L: 2 yds (1.7 m) XL: 2 yds (1.8 m)
- 41" (104 cm)

For H

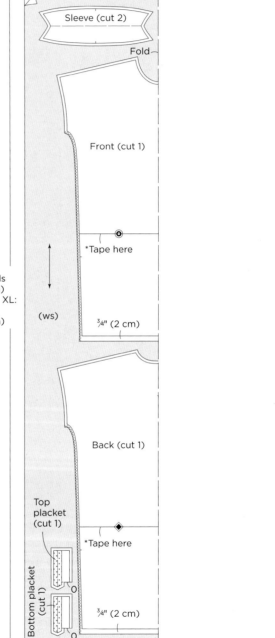

For H diagram labels:
- Outside collar — ⅜" (1 cm)
- Collar (cut 1)
- Sleeve (cut 2)
- Fold
- Front (cut 1)
- *Tape here
- ¾" (2 cm)
- (ws)
- S: 2 ¾ yds (2.5 m) M, L & XL: 3 yds (2.6 m)
- Back (cut 1)
- Top placket (cut 1)
- *Tape here
- Bottom placket (cut 1)
- ¾" (2 cm)
- 41" (104 cm)

- Add ⅜" (1 cm) seam allowance, unless otherwise noted.
- Do not add seam allowance to areas marked 0.
- Use an overlock machine to finish the raw edges of the front and back, as shown in the above diagrams.
- Cut out and adhere fusible interfacing to the wrong side of the fabric for the areas shaded with ▒▒▒.

Construction Steps

1. Make the placket (see page 112).

2. Sew the shoulders (see page 113).

3. Make the collar (see page 113).

4. Sew the side seams and make the slit (see page 114).

5. Make the sleeves (see page 115).

6. Hem the bottom (see page 115).

7. Make the buttonholes and attach the buttons (refer to the pattern for placement).

Sew using ⅜" (1 cm) seam allowance, unless otherwise noted.

G

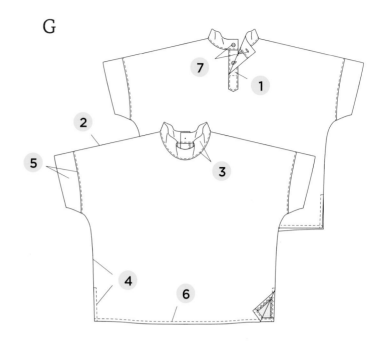

H

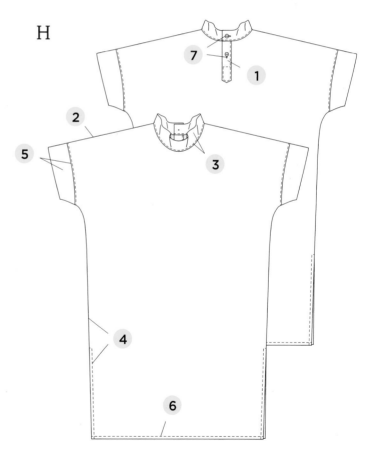

1 Make the placket

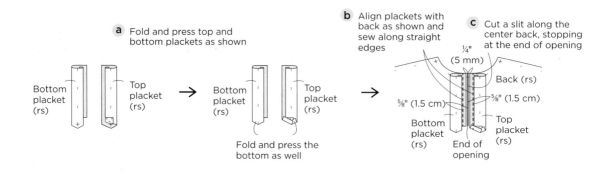

a Fold and press top and bottom plackets as shown

Bottom placket (rs)   Top placket (rs)

→

Bottom placket (rs)   Top placket (rs)

Fold and press the bottom as well

→

b Align plackets with back as shown and sew along straight edges

c Cut a slit along the center back, stopping at the end of opening

¼" (5 mm)

Back (rs)

⅝" (1.5 cm)   ⅝" (1.5 cm)

Bottom placket (rs)   End of opening   Top placket (rs)

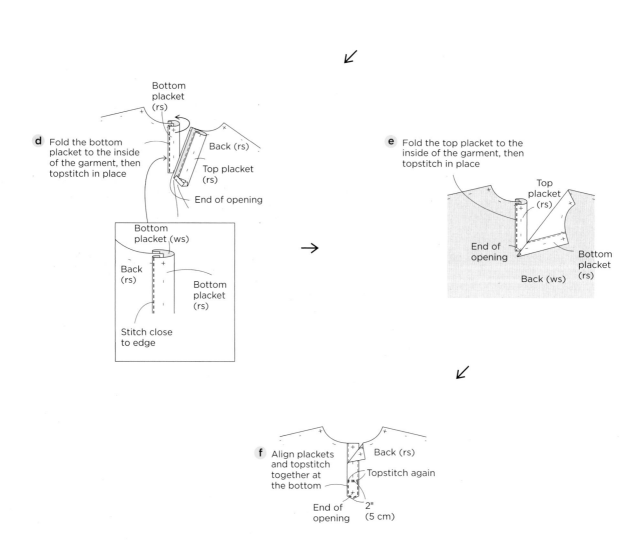

d Fold the bottom placket to the inside of the garment, then topstitch in place

Bottom placket (rs)

Back (rs)

Top placket (rs)

End of opening

Bottom placket (ws)

Back (rs)

Bottom placket (rs)

Stitch close to edge

→

e Fold the top placket to the inside of the garment, then topstitch in place

Top placket (rs)

End of opening

Back (ws)

Bottom placket (rs)

f Align plackets and topstitch together at the bottom

Back (rs)

Topstitch again

End of opening   2" (5 cm)

2 Sew the shoulders

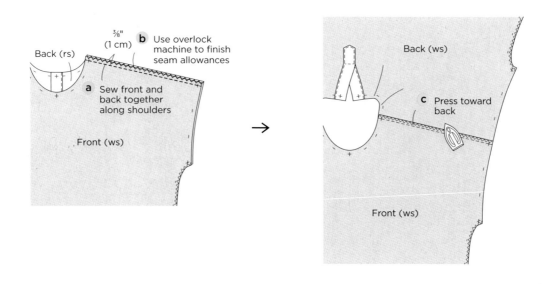

3/8" (1 cm)

b Use overlock machine to finish seam allowances

Back (rs)

a Sew front and back together along shoulders

Front (ws)

Back (ws)

c Press toward back

Front (ws)

3 Make the collar

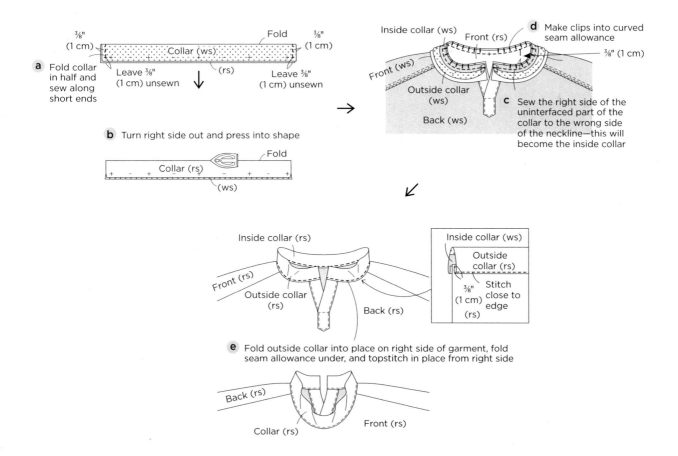

3/8" (1 cm) Fold **3/8" (1 cm)**

Collar (ws)

a Fold collar in half and sew along short ends

Leave 3/8" (1 cm) unsewn   (rs)   Leave 3/8" (1 cm) unsewn

b Turn right side out and press into shape

Fold

Collar (rs)

(ws)

Inside collar (ws)   Front (rs)   **d** Make clips into curved seam allowance

3/8" (1 cm)

Front (ws)

Outside collar (ws)

Back (ws)

c Sew the right side of the uninterfaced part of the collar to the wrong side of the neckline—this will become the inside collar

Inside collar (rs)

Front (rs)

Outside collar (rs)

Back (rs)

Inside collar (ws)

Outside collar (rs)

3/8" (1 cm)   Stitch close to edge

(rs)

e Fold outside collar into place on right side of garment, fold seam allowance under, and topstitch in place from right side

Back (rs)

Collar (rs)   Front (rs)

4 Sew the side seams and make the slit

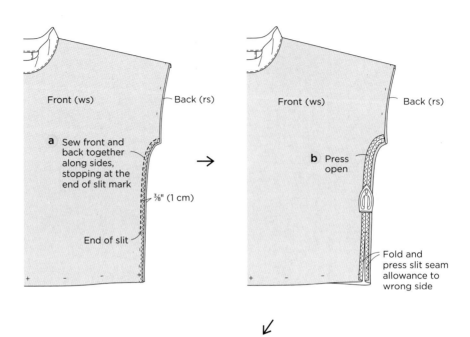

Front (ws) — Back (rs)

a Sew front and back together along sides, stopping at the end of slit mark

⅜" (1 cm)

End of slit

Front (ws) — Back (rs)

b Press open

Fold and press slit seam allowance to wrong side

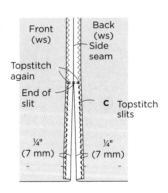

Front (ws) Back (ws)
Side seam

Topstitch again

End of slit

c Topstitch slits

¼" (7 mm) ¼" (7 mm)

5 Make the sleeves

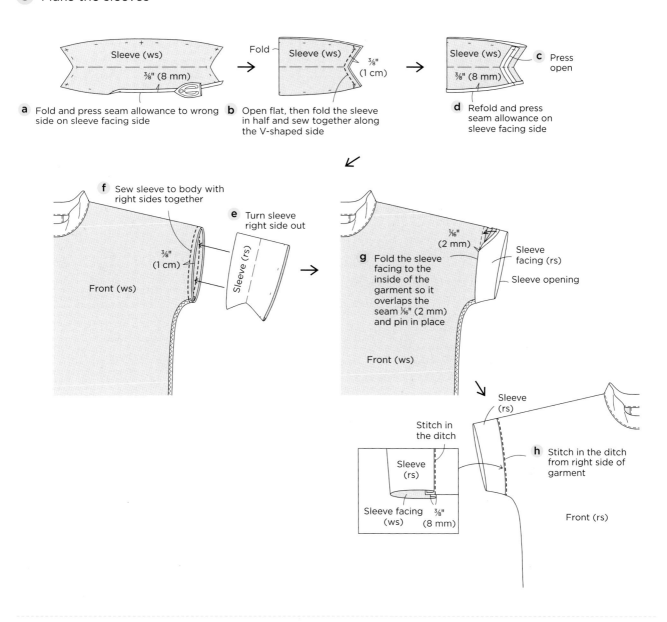

a Fold and press seam allowance to wrong side on sleeve facing side

Sleeve (ws)

³⁄₈" (8 mm)

b Open flat, then fold the sleeve in half and sew together along the V-shaped side

Fold

Sleeve (ws)

³⁄₈" (1 cm)

c Press open

Sleeve (ws)

³⁄₈" (8 mm)

d Refold and press seam allowance on sleeve facing side

f Sew sleeve to body with right sides together

Front (ws)

³⁄₈" (1 cm)

e Turn sleeve right side out

Sleeve (rs)

g Fold the sleeve facing to the inside of the garment so it overlaps the seam ¹⁄₁₆" (2 mm) and pin in place

¹⁄₁₆" (2 mm)

Sleeve facing (rs)

Sleeve opening

Front (ws)

Stitch in the ditch

Sleeve (rs)

Sleeve facing (ws)

³⁄₈" (8 mm)

h Stitch in the ditch from right side of garment

Front (rs)

6 Hem the bottom

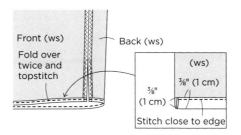

Front (ws)

Fold over twice and topstitch

Back (ws)

(ws)

³⁄₈" (1 cm)

³⁄₈" (1 cm)

Stitch close to edge

N | Cache-Cœur Short Sleeve Dress

Shown on page 13

O | Cache-Cœur Coat

Shown on pages 36 and 37

Finished Sizes

	S	M	L	XL
Bust	41" (104.2 cm)	43" (109.4 cm)	44 ¾" (113.4 cm)	47" (119.4 cm)
Sleeve Length (for O only)	14 ¼" (36 cm)	14 ½" (37 cm)	15" (38 cm)	15 ½" (31 cm)
Length	41" (104 cm)	41 ½" (105.5 cm)	42 ¼" (107.5 cm)	43 ¼" (109.5 cm)

Materials

For Both

- 41" (104 cm) wide linen or cotton/linen blend (see chart at right for yardage)
- 25 ½" x 8" (65 x 20 cm) of fusible interfacing
- One ⅜" (1 cm) diameter button
- Two ¾" (2 cm) diameter buttons

For N

	S	M	L	XL
Fabric Requirements	3 ¾ yds (3.4 m)	4 yds (3.5 m)	4 yds (3.5 m)	4 yds (3.5 m)

For O

	S	M	L	XL
Fabric Requirements	3 ¾ yds (3.4 m)	4 yds (3.5 m)	4 yds (3.5 m)	4 yds (3.6 m)

Pattern Pieces on Sheet 3

- ☐ Front*
- ☐ Back*
- ☐ Sleeve (for O only)
- ☐ Pocket
- ☐ Back facing
- ☐ Front facing
- ☐ Belt loop
- ☐ Buttonhole fabric

*Note that both the front and back are divided into two pieces in order to fit on the pattern sheet, and will need to be taped together for the complete pattern.

There are no pattern pieces for the belt and button loop. Cut following the dimensions listed below:

- ☐ Button loop (cut 1 on the bias): 2" x ¾" (5 x 1.8 cm)

	S	M	L	XL
Belt	4" x 76" (10 x 193 cm)	4" x 78" (10 x 198 cm)	4" x 79 ½" (10 x 202 cm)	4" x 82" (10 x 208 cm)

Pattern Layout

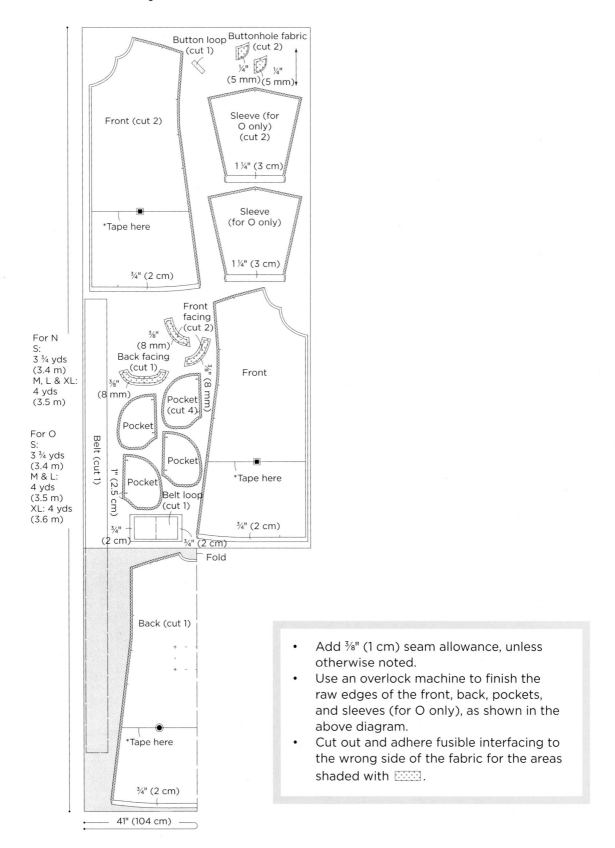

Button loop (cut 1)

Buttonhole fabric (cut 2)

¼" (5 mm) ¼" (5 mm)

Front (cut 2)

Sleeve (for O only) (cut 2)

1 ¼" (3 cm)

*Tape here

Sleeve (for O only)

1 ¼" (3 cm)

¾" (2 cm)

For N
S:
3 ¾ yds
(3.4 m)
M, L & XL:
4 yds
(3.5 m)

For O
S:
3 ¾ yds
(3.4 m)
M & L:
4 yds
(3.5 m)
XL: 4 yds
(3.6 m)

Front facing (cut 2)

⅜" (8 mm)

Back facing (cut 1)

⅜" (8 mm)

⅜" (8 mm)

Front

Pocket (cut 4)

Pocket

Pocket

Pocket

Belt loop (cut 1)

Belt (cut 1)

1" (2.5 cm)

*Tape here

¾" (2 cm)

¾" (2 cm)

¾" (2 cm)

Fold

Back (cut 1)

*Tape here

¾" (2 cm)

41" (104 cm)

- Add ⅜" (1 cm) seam allowance, unless otherwise noted.
- Use an overlock machine to finish the raw edges of the front, back, pockets, and sleeves (for O only), as shown in the above diagram.
- Cut out and adhere fusible interfacing to the wrong side of the fabric for the areas shaded with ▒▒▒.

Construction Steps

1. Make the belt loop and attach it to the back (see page 119).

2. Sew the shoulders (see step 2 on page 99).

3. Make the pockets and sew the sides (see step 6 on page 107). Do not fold and press the sleeve opening seam allowance to the wrong side for O.

4. For N, finish the sleeve opening (see step 7 on page 108). For O, make the sleeves (see page 119).

5. Make the button loop and attach it to the right front (see page 119).

6. Make the facing (see page 120).

7. Make the buttonholes and attach to the front (see page 120).

8. Finish the front edge, securing the facing and buttonholes (see page 121).

9. Hem the bottom.

10. Attach the buttons (see pattern for placement).

11. Make the belt and insert through the belt loop (see page 121).

Sew using ⅜" (1 cm) seam allowance, unless otherwise noted.

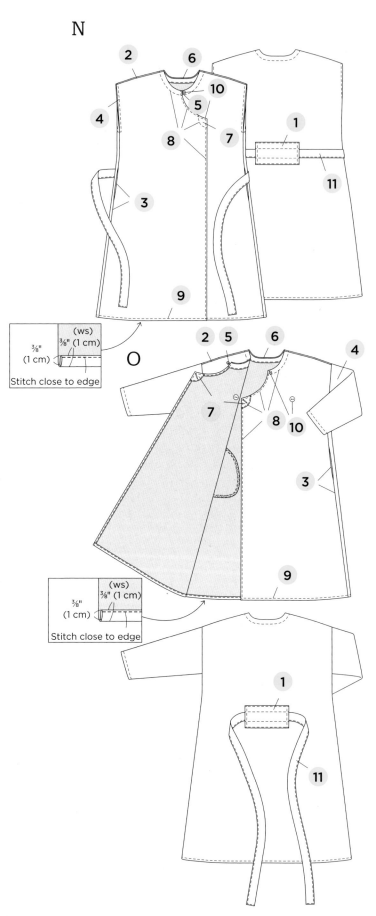

1 Make the belt loop and attach it to the back

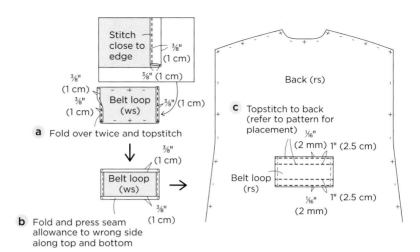

a Fold over twice and topstitch

Stitch close to edge
⅜" (1 cm)
⅜" (1 cm)

⅜" (1 cm)
⅜" (1 cm)
Belt loop (ws)
⅜" (1 cm)

⅜" (1 cm)
Belt loop (ws)
⅜" (1 cm)

b Fold and press seam allowance to wrong side along top and bottom

Back (rs)

c Topstitch to back (refer to pattern for placement)
1/16" (2 mm) 1" (2.5 cm)

Belt loop (rs)

1/16" (2 mm) 1" (2.5 cm)

4 For O, make the sleeves

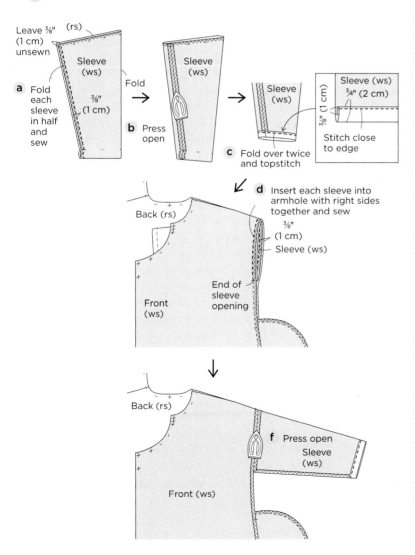

Leave ⅜" (1 cm) unsewn
(rs)

a Fold each sleeve in half and sew
Sleeve (ws)
⅜" (1 cm)

Fold
Sleeve (ws)

b Press open

Sleeve (ws)

Sleeve (ws)
¾" (2 cm)
⅜" (1 cm)

c Fold over twice and topstitch

Stitch close to edge

d Insert each sleeve into armhole with right sides together and sew

Back (rs)

⅜" (1 cm)
Sleeve (ws)

End of sleeve opening

Front (ws)

Back (rs)

f Press open
Sleeve (ws)

Front (ws)

5 Make the button loop and attach it to the left front

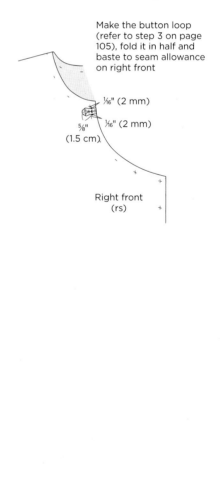

Make the button loop (refer to step 3 on page 105), fold it in half and baste to seam allowance on right front

1/16" (2 mm)
⅝" (1.5 cm)
1/16" (2 mm)

Right front (rs)

6 Make the facing

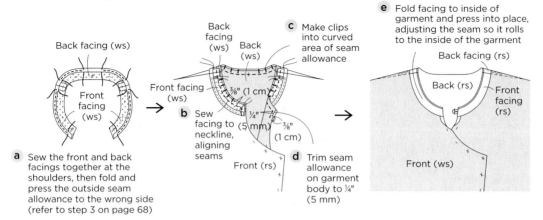

e Fold facing to inside of garment and press into place, adjusting the seam so it rolls to the inside of the garment

Back facing (ws)

Front facing (ws)

Back facing (ws)

Back (ws)

c Make clips into curved area of seam allowance

Front facing (ws)

⅜" (1 cm)

b Sew facing to neckline, aligning seams

¼" (5 mm)

⅜" (1 cm)

Front (rs)

d Trim seam allowance on garment body to ¼" (5 mm)

a Sew the front and back facings together at the shoulders, then fold and press the outside seam allowance to the wrong side (refer to step 3 on page 68)

Back facing (rs)

Back (rs)

Front facing (rs)

Front (ws)

7 Make the buttonholes and attach to the front

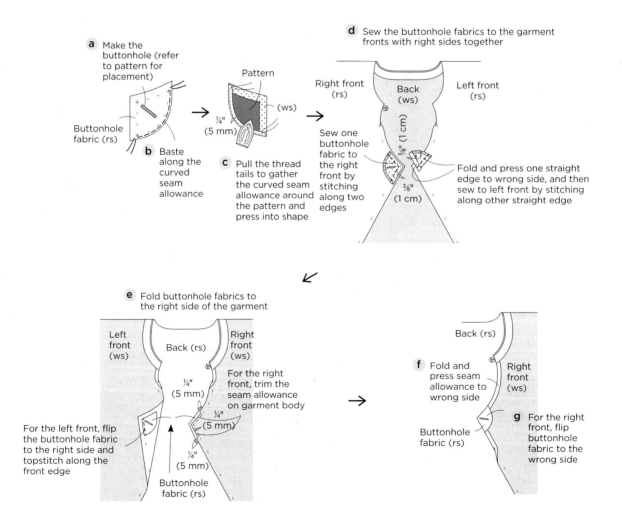

a Make the buttonhole (refer to pattern for placement)

Buttonhole fabric (rs)

b Baste along the curved seam allowance

Pattern

¼" (5 mm)

(ws)

c Pull the thread tails to gather the curved seam allowance around the pattern and press into shape

d Sew the buttonhole fabrics to the garment fronts with right sides together

Right front (rs)

Back (ws)

Left front (rs)

⅜" (1 cm)

⅜" (1 cm)

Sew one buttonhole fabric to the right front by stitching along two edges

Fold and press one straight edge to wrong side, and then sew to left front by stitching along other straight edge

e Fold buttonhole fabrics to the right side of the garment

Left front (ws)

Back (rs)

Right front (ws)

¼" (5 mm)

For the right front, trim the seam allowance on garment body

¼" (5 mm)

¼" (5 mm)

For the left front, flip the buttonhole fabric to the right side and topstitch along the front edge

Buttonhole fabric (rs)

Back (rs)

f Fold and press seam allowance to wrong side

Right front (ws)

Buttonhole fabric (rs)

g For the right front, flip buttonhole fabric to the wrong side

8 Finish the front edge, securing the facing and buttonholes

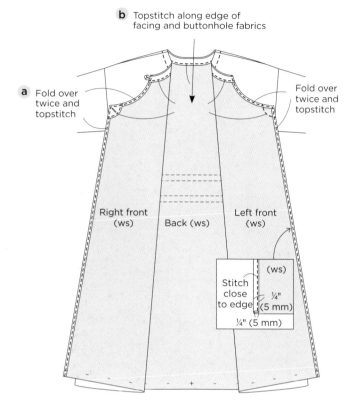

b Topstitch along edge of facing and buttonhole fabrics

a Fold over twice and topstitch

Fold over twice and topstitch

Right front (ws)

Back (ws)

Left front (ws)

Stitch close to edge

¼" (5 mm)

(ws)

¼" (5 mm)

11 Make the belt and insert through the belt loop

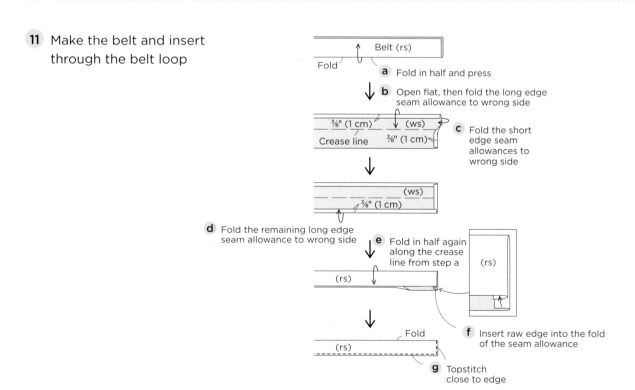

Belt (rs)

Fold

a Fold in half and press

b Open flat, then fold the long edge seam allowance to wrong side

⅜" (1 cm)

Crease line

(ws)

⅜" (1 cm)

c Fold the short edge seam allowances to wrong side

(ws)

⅜" (1 cm)

d Fold the remaining long edge seam allowance to wrong side

e Fold in half again along the crease line from step a

(rs)

(rs)

f Insert raw edge into the fold of the seam allowance

Fold

(rs)

g Topstitch close to edge

P | Cook's Dress

Shown on pages 17, 22 and 24

Finished Sizes

	S	M	L	XL
Bust	42 ¼" (107.2 cm)	44" (112 cm)	45 ¾" (116 cm)	48" (122 cm)
Sleeve Length	15" (38 cm)	15 ½" (39 cm)	15 ¾" (40 cm)	16 ¼" (41 cm)
Length	43 ¼" (109.5 cm)	43 ¾" (111 cm)	44 ½" (113 cm)	45 ¼" (115 cm)

Materials

- 41" (104 cm) wide cotton silk, cotton double gauze, or linen (see chart below for yardage)
- 35 ½" x 11 ¾" (90 x 30 cm) of fusible interfacing
- ½" (1.2 cm) wide stay tape (see chart below for length)
- Two ⅜" (1 cm) diameter buttons

	S	M	L	XL
Fabric Requirements	4 yds (3.6 m)	4 yds (3.6 m)	4 yds (3.6 m)	4 ¼ yds (3.7 m)
Stay Tape Requirements	2 yds (1.8 m)	2 ¼ yds (1.9 m)	2 ¼ yds (2 m)	2 ½ yds (2.1 m)

Pattern Pieces on Sheet 2

- ☐ Front
- ☐ Back
- ☐ Center front panel
- ☐ Front skirt
- ☐ Back skirt
- ☐ Sleeve
- ☐ Pocket
- ☐ Collar
- ☐ Front waistband
- ☐ Back waistband

There are no pattern pieces for the button loop. Cut following the dimensions listed below:

- ☐ Button loop (cut 1 on the bias): 5 ¼" x ¾" (13 x 1.8 cm)

Pattern Layout

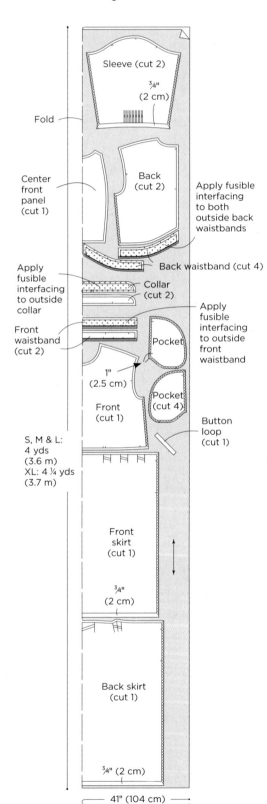

Sleeve (cut 2)
¾" (2 cm)

Fold

Back (cut 2)

Center front panel (cut 1)

Apply fusible interfacing to both outside back waistbands

Back waistband (cut 4)

Apply fusible interfacing to outside collar

Collar (cut 2)

Front waistband (cut 2)

Apply fusible interfacing to outside front waistband

Pocket

Pocket (cut 4)

1" (2.5 cm)

Front (cut 1)

Button loop (cut 1)

S, M & L: 4 yds (3.6 m)
XL: 4 ¼ yds (3.7 m)

Front skirt (cut 1)

¾" (2 cm)

Back skirt (cut 1)

¾" (2 cm)

← 41" (104 cm) →

- Add ⅜" (1 cm) seam allowance, unless otherwise noted.
- Use an overlock machine to finish the raw edges of the front, back, front skirt, back skirt, pockets, and sleeves, as shown in the diagram on page 122.
- Cut out and adhere fusible interfacing to the wrong side of the fabric for the areas shaded with ▨.
- Adhere or sew stay tape to the wrong side of the fabric for the areas shaded with ▨.

Construction Steps

1 Attach center front panel to front bodice (see page 124).

2 Sew the back bodices together and make the button loops (see steps 2 [f and g only] and 3 on pages 104 and 105).

3 Sew the shoulders (see step 4 [e-g only] on page 105).

4 Make the collar (see step 5 on page 106).

5 Sew the bodice side seams (see page 124).

6 Make the waistbands (see page 124).

7 Attach the waistbands to the bodice (see page 125).

8 Make the tucks on the front skirt (see page 125).

9 Make the pockets and sew the skirt side seams (see page 125).

10 Make the tucks on the back skirt and attach the waistbands (see page 126).

11 Make the sleeves (see page 127).

12 Hem the dress.

13 Attach the buttons (refer to pattern for placement).

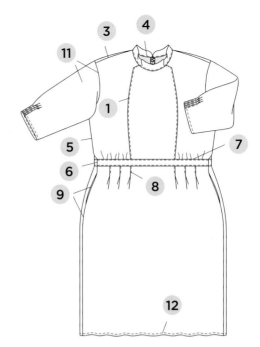

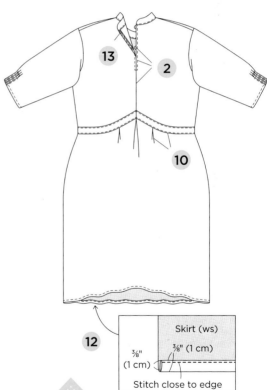

Skirt (ws)

⅜" (1 cm)

⅜" (1 cm)

Stitch close to edge

Sew using ⅜" (1 cm) seam allowance, unless otherwise noted.

1 Attach center front panel to front bodice

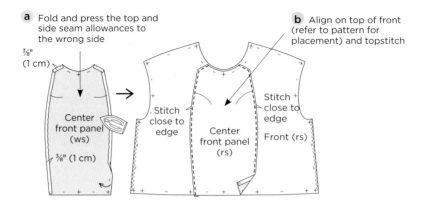

a Fold and press the top and side seam allowances to the wrong side

⅜" (1 cm)

Center front panel (ws)

⅜" (1 cm)

b Align on top of front (refer to pattern for placement) and topstitch

Stitch close to edge

Stitch close to edge

Center front panel (rs)

Front (rs)

---

5 Sew the bodice side seams

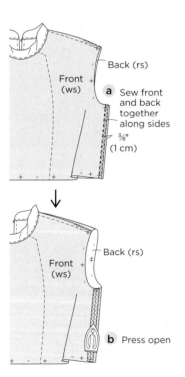

Back (rs)

Front (ws)

a Sew front and back together along sides

⅜" (1 cm)

Back (rs)

Front (ws)

b Press open

6 Make the waistbands (both outside and inside)

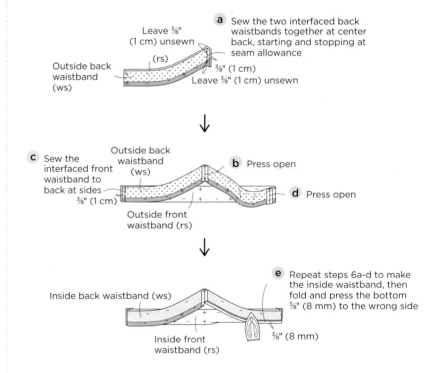

Leave ⅜" (1 cm) unsewn

(rs)

Outside back waistband (ws)

a Sew the two interfaced back waistbands together at center back, starting and stopping at seam allowance

⅜" (1 cm)

Leave ⅜" (1 cm) unsewn

c Sew the interfaced front waistband to back at sides ⅜" (1 cm)

Outside back waistband (ws)

b Press open

d Press open

Outside front waistband (rs)

Inside back waistband (ws)

Inside front waistband (rs)

e Repeat steps 6a-d to make the inside waistband, then fold and press the bottom ⅜" (8 mm) to the wrong side

⅜" (8 mm)

7 Attach the waistbands to the bodice

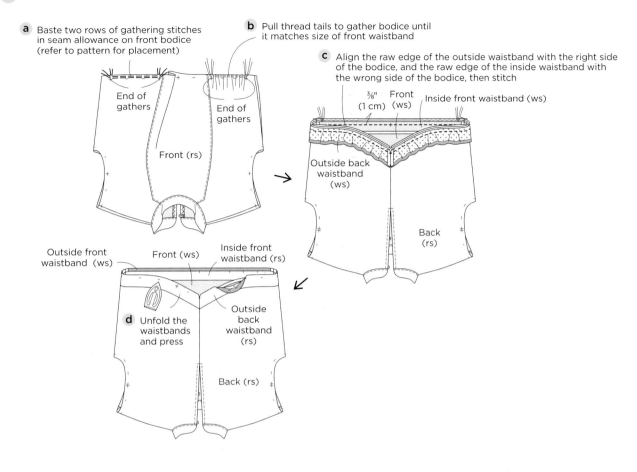

a Baste two rows of gathering stitches in seam allowance on front bodice (refer to pattern for placement)

End of gathers

End of gathers

Front (rs)

b Pull thread tails to gather bodice until it matches size of front waistband

c Align the raw edge of the outside waistband with the right side of the bodice, and the raw edge of the inside waistband with the wrong side of the bodice, then stitch

⅜" (1 cm)

Front (ws)

Inside front waistband (ws)

Outside back waistband (ws)

Back (rs)

Outside front waistband (ws)

Front (ws)

Inside front waistband (rs)

d Unfold the waistbands and press

Outside back waistband (rs)

Back (rs)

8 Make the tucks on the front skirt

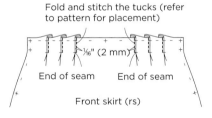

Fold and stitch the tucks (refer to pattern for placement)

1⁄16" (2 mm)

End of seam

End of seam

Front skirt (rs)

9 Make the pockets and sew the skirt side seams

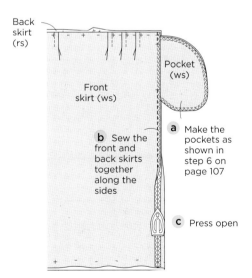

Back skirt (rs)

Front skirt (ws)

Pocket (ws)

a Make the pockets as shown in step 6 on page 107

b Sew the front and back skirts together along the sides

c Press open

10 Make the tucks on the back skirt and attach the waistbands

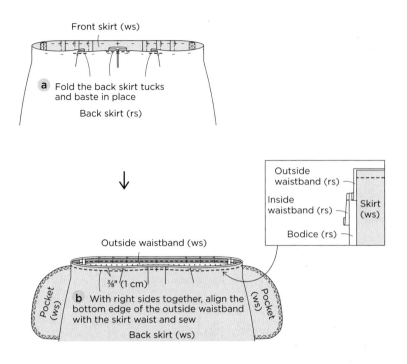

Front skirt (ws)

a Fold the back skirt tucks and baste in place

Back skirt (rs)

↓

Outside waistband (ws)

Outside waistband (rs)

Inside waistband (rs)

Skirt (ws)

Bodice (rs)

⅜" (1 cm)

Pocket (ws)

Pocket (ws)

b With right sides together, align the bottom edge of the outside waistband with the skirt waist and sew

Back skirt (ws)

↘

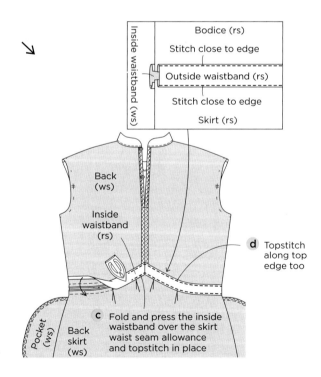

Inside waistband (ws)

Bodice (rs)

Stitch close to edge

Outside waistband (rs)

Stitch close to edge

Skirt (rs)

Back (ws)

Inside waistband (rs)

d Topstitch along top edge too

Pocket (ws)

Back skirt (ws)

c Fold and press the inside waistband over the skirt waist seam allowance and topstitch in place

11 Make the sleeves

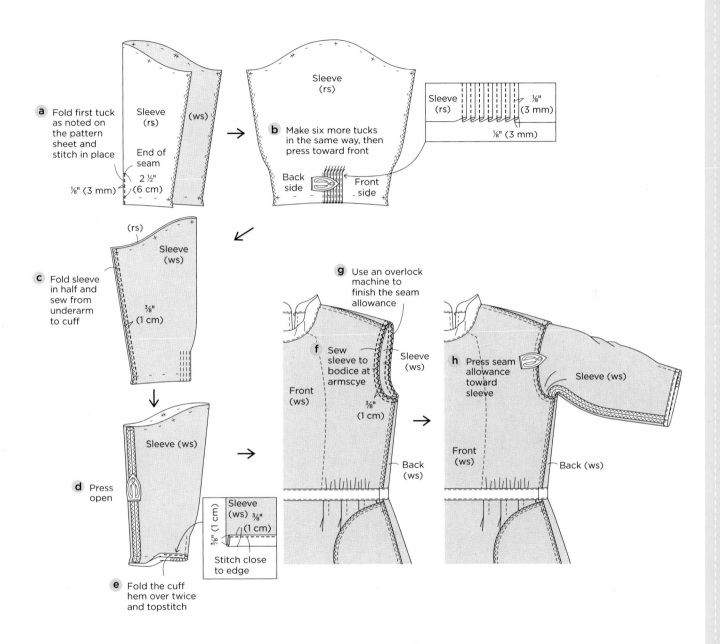

a Fold first tuck as noted on the pattern sheet and stitch in place

⅛" (3 mm)

Sleeve (rs)

(ws)

End of seam

2 ½" (6 cm)

Sleeve (rs)

b Make six more tucks in the same way, then press toward front

Back side

Front side

Sleeve (rs)

⅛" (3 mm)

⅛" (3 mm)

c Fold sleeve in half and sew from underarm to cuff

(rs)

Sleeve (ws)

⅜" (1 cm)

d Press open

Sleeve (ws)

e Fold the cuff hem over twice and topstitch

Sleeve (ws) ⅜" (1 cm)

⅜" (1 cm)

Stitch close to edge

f Sew sleeve to bodice at armscye

g Use an overlock machine to finish the seam allowance

Sleeve (ws)

Front (ws)

⅜" (1 cm)

Back (ws)

h Press seam allowance toward sleeve

Sleeve (ws)

Front (ws)

Back (ws)

Q | Short Sleeve Gathered Dress

Shown on page 31

R | Long Sleeve Gathered Dress

Shown on pages 32, 42 and 46

Finished Sizes

	S	M	L	XL
Bust	62 ½" (158.8 cm)	64 ½" (164 cm)	66 ¼" (168 cm)	68 ½" (174 cm)
Sleeve Length (for R only)	20 ½" (52 cm)	21" (53 cm)	21 ¼" (54 cm)	21 ¾" (55 cm)
Length	47 ¾" (121.5 cm)	48 ½" (123 cm)	49 ¼" (125 cm)	50" (127 cm)

Materials

For Q

- 41" (104 cm) wide linen (see chart at right for yardage)
- Fusible interfacing (see chart at right for dimensions)
- 39 ½" (100 cm) of ½" (1.2 cm) wide single fold bias tape

For Q

	S	M	L	XL
Fabric Requirements	4 ⅜ yds (3.9 m)	4 ⅜ yds (3.9 m)	4 ⅜ yds (3.9 m)	4 ½ yds (4 m)
Fusible Interfacing Requirements	4" x 6" (10 x 15 cm)	4" x 8" (10 x 20 cm)	4" x 8" (10 x 20 cm)	4" x 8" (10 x 20 cm)

For R

- 41" (104 cm) wide lyocell or linen (see chart at right for yardage)
- Fusible interfacing (see chart at right for dimensions)
- Four ⅜" (1 cm) diameter buttons

For R

	S	M	L	XL
Fabric Requirements	4 ¾ yds (4.2 m)	4 ¾ yds (4.3 m)	4 ¾ yds (4.3 m)	5 yds (4.4 m)
Fusible Interfacing Requirements	17 ¾" x 9 ¾" (45 x 25 cm)	17 ¾" x 9 ¾" (45 x 25 cm)	17 ¾" x 11 ¾" (45 x 30 cm)	17 ¾" x 11 ¾" (45 x 30 cm)

Pattern Pieces on Sheet 5

- ☐ Front*
- ☐ Back*
- ☐ Front yoke
- ☐ Back yoke
- ☐ Pocket
- ☐ Placket
- ☐ Tie collar
- ☐ Sleeve (for R only)
- ☐ Cuff (for R only)

*Note that both the front and back are divided into two pieces in order to fit on the pattern sheet, and will need to be taped together for the complete pattern.

Pattern Layout

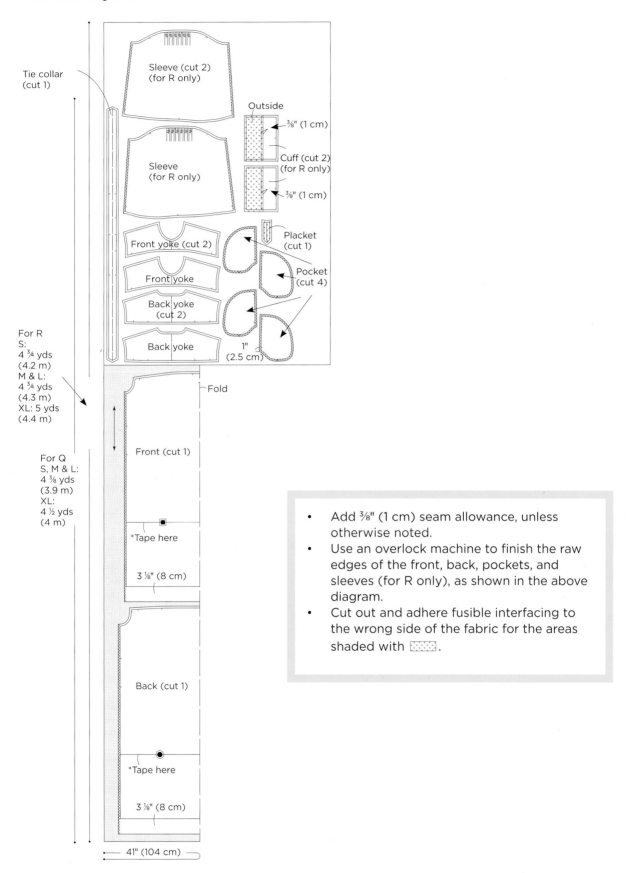

Tie collar (cut 1)

Sleeve (cut 2) (for R only)

Sleeve (for R only)

Outside

⅜" (1 cm)

Cuff (cut 2) (for R only)

⅜" (1 cm)

Front yoke (cut 2)

Front yoke

Back yoke (cut 2)

Back yoke

Placket (cut 1)

Pocket (cut 4)

1" (2.5 cm)

For R
S:
4 ¾ yds (4.2 m)
M & L:
4 ¾ yds (4.3 m)
XL: 5 yds (4.4 m)

For Q
S, M & L:
4 ⅜ yds (3.9 m)
XL:
4 ½ yds (4 m)

Fold

Front (cut 1)

*Tape here

3 ⅛" (8 cm)

Back (cut 1)

*Tape here

3 ⅛" (8 cm)

41" (104 cm)

- Add ⅜" (1 cm) seam allowance, unless otherwise noted.
- Use an overlock machine to finish the raw edges of the front, back, pockets, and sleeves (for R only), as shown in the above diagram.
- Cut out and adhere fusible interfacing to the wrong side of the fabric for the areas shaded with ▒.

Construction Steps

1. Gather the front and sew it to the front yoke (see page 131).

2. Make the placket (see page 131).

3. Gather the back and sew it to the back yoke (see page 132).

4. Sew the front and back yokes together at the shoulders and finish the inside back yoke (see page 132).

5. Attach the tie collar (see page 133).

6. For Q, finish the sleeve openings with bias tape (see page 133). For R, make the pockets and sew the side seams (see step 6 on page 107).

7. For Q, make the pockets and sew the side seams (see page 134). For R, make the sleeves (see pages 134-135).

8. Hem the dress (see page 135).

Sew using
⅜" (1 cm) seam
allowance, unless
otherwise
noted.

Q

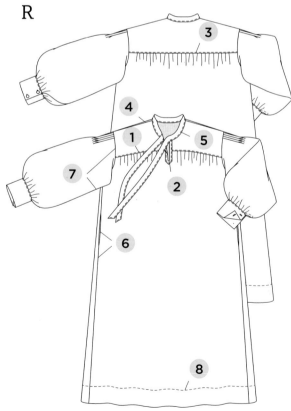

R

1 Gather the front and sew it to the front yoke

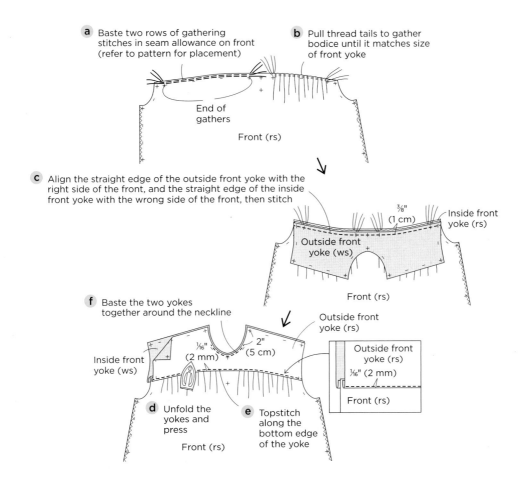

a Baste two rows of gathering stitches in seam allowance on front (refer to pattern for placement)

b Pull thread tails to gather bodice until it matches size of front yoke

End of gathers

Front (rs)

c Align the straight edge of the outside front yoke with the right side of the front, and the straight edge of the inside front yoke with the wrong side of the front, then stitch

⅜" (1 cm)

Inside front yoke (rs)

Outside front yoke (ws)

Front (rs)

f Baste the two yokes together around the neckline

Outside front yoke (rs)

Inside front yoke (ws)

1/16" (2 mm)

2" (5 cm)

Outside front yoke (rs)

1/16" (2 mm)

Front (rs)

d Unfold the yokes and press

e Topstitch along the bottom edge of the yoke

Front (rs)

2 Make the placket

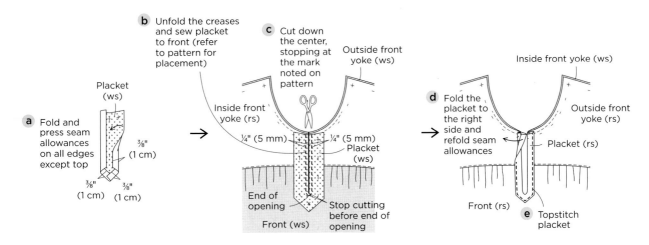

a Fold and press seam allowances on all edges except top

Placket (ws)

⅜" (1 cm)

⅜" (1 cm)   ⅜" (1 cm)

b Unfold the creases and sew placket to front (refer to pattern for placement)

c Cut down the center, stopping at the mark noted on pattern

Inside front yoke (rs)

Outside front yoke (ws)

¼" (5 mm)   ¼" (5 mm) Placket (ws)

End of opening

Front (ws)

Stop cutting before end of opening

d Fold the placket to the right side and refold seam allowances

Inside front yoke (ws)

Outside front yoke (rs)

Placket (rs)

Front (rs)

e Topstitch placket

3 Gather the back and sew it to the back yoke

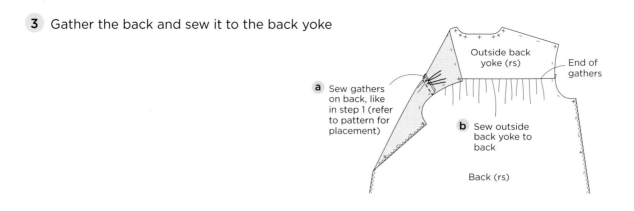

a Sew gathers on back, like in step 1 (refer to pattern for placement)

Outside back yoke (rs)

End of gathers

b Sew outside back yoke to back

Back (rs)

---

4 Sew the front and back yokes together at the shoulders and finish the inside back yoke

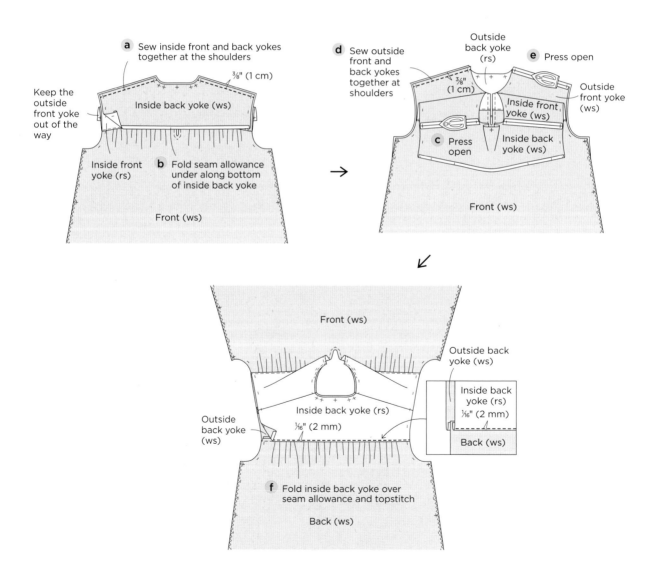

a Sew inside front and back yokes together at the shoulders

⅜" (1 cm)

Keep the outside front yoke out of the way

Inside back yoke (ws)

Inside front yoke (rs)

b Fold seam allowance under along bottom of inside back yoke

Front (ws)

d Sew outside front and back yokes together at shoulders

Outside back yoke (rs)

⅜" (1 cm)

e Press open

Outside front yoke (ws)

Inside front yoke (ws)

c Press open

Inside back yoke (ws)

Front (ws)

Front (ws)

Outside back yoke (ws)

Outside back yoke (ws)

Inside back yoke (rs)

1/16" (2 mm)

Inside back yoke (rs)

1/16" (2 mm)

Back (ws)

f Fold inside back yoke over seam allowance and topstitch

Back (ws)

5 | Attach the tie collar

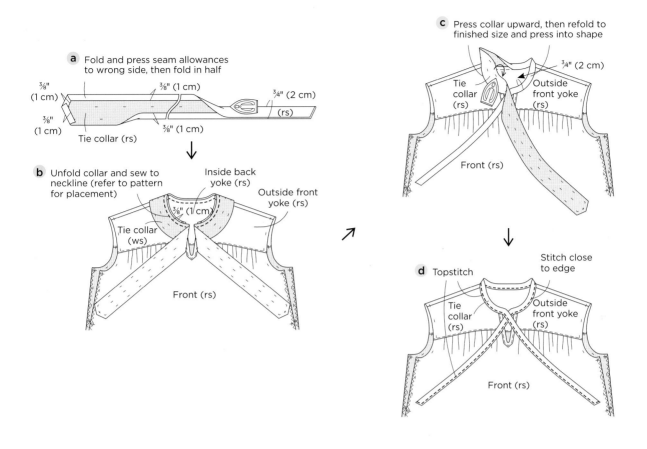

a Fold and press seam allowances to wrong side, then fold in half

⅜" (1 cm)

⅜" (1 cm)

⅜" (1 cm)

⅜" (1 cm)

¾" (2 cm)

(rs)

Tie collar (rs)

b Unfold collar and sew to neckline (refer to pattern for placement)

Inside back yoke (rs)

Outside front yoke (rs)

⅜" (1 cm)

Tie collar (ws)

Front (rs)

c Press collar upward, then refold to finished size and press into shape

¾" (2 cm)

Tie collar (rs)

Outside front yoke (rs)

Front (rs)

d Topstitch

Stitch close to edge

Tie collar (rs)

Outside front yoke (rs)

Front (rs)

6 | For Q, finish the sleeve openings with bias tape

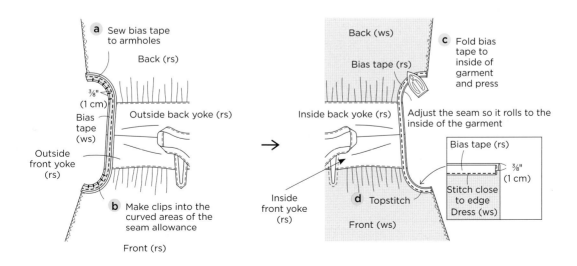

a Sew bias tape to armholes

Back (rs)

⅜" (1 cm)

Bias tape (ws)

Outside back yoke (rs)

Outside front yoke (rs)

b Make clips into the curved areas of the seam allowance

Front (rs)

Back (ws)

Bias tape (rs)

c Fold bias tape to inside of garment and press

Inside back yoke (rs)

Adjust the seam so it rolls to the inside of the garment

Inside front yoke (rs)

d Topstitch

Front (ws)

Bias tape (rs)

⅜" (1 cm)

Stitch close to edge

Dress (ws)

7 For Q, make the pockets and sew the side seams

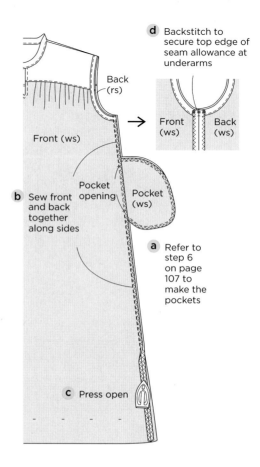

d Backstitch to secure top edge of seam allowance at underarms

Back (rs)

Front (ws)

b Sew front and back together along sides

Pocket opening

Pocket (ws)

Front (ws) Back (ws)

a Refer to step 6 on page 107 to make the pockets

c Press open

For R, make the sleeves

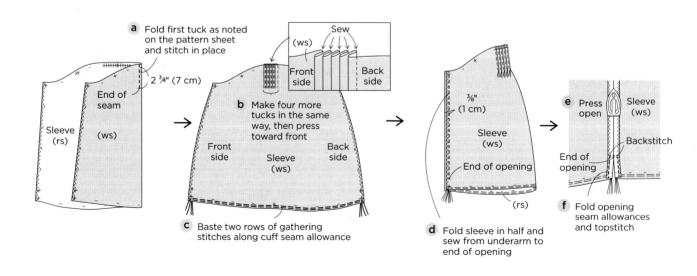

a Fold first tuck as noted on the pattern sheet and stitch in place

2 ¾" (7 cm)

End of seam

Sleeve (rs) (ws)

Sew

(ws)

Front side Back side

b Make four more tucks in the same way, then press toward front

Front side Sleeve (ws) Back side

c Baste two rows of gathering stitches along cuff seam allowance

⅜" (1 cm)

Sleeve (ws)

End of opening

(rs)

d Fold sleeve in half and sew from underarm to end of opening

e Press open

Sleeve (ws)

Backstitch

End of opening

f Fold opening seam allowances and topstitch

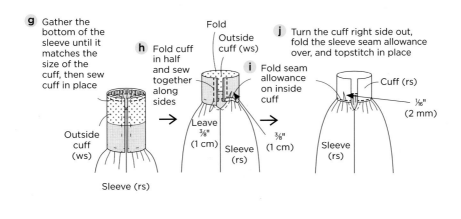

g Gather the bottom of the sleeve until it matches the size of the cuff, then sew cuff in place

Outside cuff (ws)

Sleeve (rs)

h Fold cuff in half and sew together along sides

Fold
Outside cuff (ws)

Leave ⅜" (1 cm)

Sleeve (rs)

i Fold seam allowance on inside cuff

⅜" (1 cm)

j Turn the cuff right side out, fold the sleeve seam allowance over, and topstitch in place

Cuff (rs)

1/16" (2 mm)

Sleeve (rs)

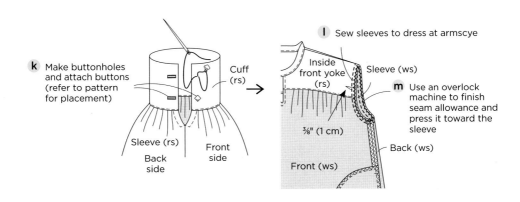

k Make buttonholes and attach buttons (refer to pattern for placement)

Cuff (rs)

Sleeve (rs)

Back side

Front side

l Sew sleeves to dress at armscye

Inside front yoke (rs)

Sleeve (ws)

m Use an overlock machine to finish seam allowance and press it toward the sleeve

⅜" (1 cm)

Back (ws)

Front (ws)

---

8 Hem the dress

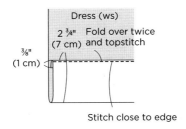

Dress (ws)

2 ¾" (7 cm) Fold over twice and topstitch

⅜" (1 cm)

Stitch close to edge

Stockists

USA

Fiddlehead Artisan Supply
www.fiddleheadartisansupply.com

Jones & Vandermeer
www.jonesandvandermeer.com

Stonemountain & Daughter Fabrics
www.stonemountainfabric.com

Superbuzzy
www.superbuzzy.com

UK

Guthrie & Ghani
www.guthrie-ghani.co.uk

Minerva
www.minerva.com

The Draper's Daughter
www.drapersdaughter.com

AUSTRALIA

Fibre Smith
www.fibresmith.com.au

Minerva's Bower
www.minervasbower.com.au

The Drapery
www.thedrapery.com.au

JAPAN

Miss Matatabi
www.shop.missmatatabi.com

SINGAPORE

Neko Neko Fabric
www.nekoneko.co

SPAIN

Nunoya
www.nunoya.com

DENMARK

Meter Meter
www.metermeter.dk

The Atelier

The Atelier to Nani Iro is located on the second floor of an old building across from Nishisemba Park in Osaka, Japan. The atelier functions as the flagship store for Nani Iro textiles, as well as a studio space for workshops and events. The knowledgeable atelier staff can assist you with choosing fabric or offer advice on sewing clothes. If you're ever in the neighborhood, please come visit us to see the fabric in person, find inspiration for your own creations, and share the joy of sewing.

The Atelier to Nani Iro
Kotobukikaikan Bldg. 2F 1-12-28
Kyomachibori, Nishi Ward, Osaka City
Website: https://atelierto.naniiro.jp
Online Shop: https://online.naniiro.jp
Instagram: @atelier_to_naniiro_textile